TEXT AND PERFORMANCE

General Editor: Michael Scott

The series is designed to introduce sixth-form and under-graduate students to the themes, continuing vitality and performance of major dramatic works. The attention given to production aspects is an element of special importance, responding to the invigoration given to literary study by the work of leading contemporary critics.

The prime aim is to present each play as a vital experience in the mind of the reader – achieved by analysis of the text in relation to its themes and theatricality. Emphasis is accordingly placed on the relevance of the work to the modern reader and the world of today. At the same time, traditional views are presented and appraised, forming the basis from which a creative response to the text can develop.

In each volume, Part One: *Text* discusses certain key themes or problems, the reader being encouraged to gain a stronger perception both of the inherent character of the work and also of variations in interpreting it. Part Two: *Performance* examines the ways in which these themes or problems have been handled in modern productions, and the approaches and techniques employed to enhance the play's accessibility to modern audiences.

A synopsis of the play is given and an outline of its major sources, and a concluding Reading List offers guidance to the student's independent study of the work.

THE MERCHANT
OF VENICE

Text and Performance

BILL OVERTON

HUMANITIES PRESS INTERNATIONAL, INC.
Atlantic Highlands, NJ

First published in 1987 in the United States of America by
HUMANITIES PRESS INTERNATIONAL, INC., Atlantic Highlands, NJ 07716

© Bill Overton 1987

LIBRARY OF CONGRESS CATALOGING IN PUBLICATION DATA
Overton, Bill.
The merchant of Venice.
(Text and performance)
Bibliography: p.
Includes index.
1. Shakespeare, William, 1564–1616. Merchant of
Venice. 2. Shakespeare, William, 1564–1616—State
history—1950–   . I. Title. II. Series.
PR2825.09   1987   822.3'3   86–18502
ISBN 0–391–03469–3 (pbk.)

PRINTED IN HONG KONG

CONTENTS

Illustrations will be found in Part Two.

ACKNOWLEDGEMENTS

All quotations from the play are from the New Penguin Shakespeare edition (1967) by W. Moelwyn Merchant. Quotations from other plays by Shakespeare are from *The Complete Works* (1951) edited by Peter Alexander.

I wish to thank the following for their help. Audio-Visual Productions Ltd and Guild Learning Ltd kindly lent me video cassettes of two televised versions of the play, and ITC Entertainment Ltd provided a copy of the script for one of them. The Theatre Museum of the Victoria and Albert Museum gave me access to reviews and the Press Office of the National Theatre showed me contact prints – their only remaining archive material – of the Jonathan Miller production. Above all, the staff of the Shakespeare Centre at Stratford-upon-Avon were unfailingly efficient and helpful.

Among individuals, I especially want to thank Jonathan Miller for discussing the play with me; Simon Shepherd for the stimulus of his 1980 production; Michael Scott, General Editor of the series and Jim Friedman, David Fussell, John Lucas and my wife Susan – all of whom read and commented on my first draft.

GENERAL EDITOR'S PREFACE

For many years a mutual suspicion existed between the theatre director and the literary critic of drama. Although in the first half of the century there were important exceptions, such was the rule. A radical change of attitude, however, has taken place over the last thirty years. Critics and directors now increasingly recognise the significance of each other's work and acknowledge their growing awareness of interdependence. Both interpret the same text, but do so according to their different situations and functions. Without the director, the designer and the actor, a play's existence is only partial. They revitalise the text with action, enabling the drama to live fully at each performance. The academic critic investigates the script to elucidate its textual problems, understand its conventions and discover how it operates. He may also propose his view of the work, expounding what he considers to be its significance.

Dramatic texts belong therefore to theatre and to literature. The aim of the 'Text and Performance' series is to achieve a fuller recognition of how both enhance our enjoyment of the play. Each volume follows the same basic pattern. Part One provides a critical introduction to the play under discussion, using the techniques and criteria of the literary critic in examining the manner in which the work operates through language, imagery and action. Part Two takes the enquiry further into the play's theatricality by focusing on selected productions of recent times so as to illustrate points of contrast and comparison in the interpretation of different directors and actors, and to demonstrate how the drama has worked on the modern stage. In this way the series seeks to provide a lively and informative introduction to major plays in their text and performance.

Michael Scott

PLOT SYNOPSIS AND SOURCES

Antonio is anxious for Bassanio who wishes to court the rich and beautiful Portia in Belmont. Bassanio needs money and Antonio promises it even though all his funds are invested in ships at sea. He borrows from Shylock, a wealthy Jew whom he has previously condemned for taking interest. Instead of paying interest Antonio agrees to forfeit a pound of his flesh if he does not repay Shylock within three months. Shylock accepts a dinner invitation to confirm the bargain. While Shylock is out his daughter Jessica elopes with Lorenzo, one of Bassanio's friends, and robs him. Shylock is grief-stricken and vows revenge.

Portia, according to her father's will, must marry the man who chooses the single casket out of three which contains her portrait. She receives many suitors, two of whom choose the gold and silver caskets and fail. Bassanio chooses the lead casket and wins her, and his friend Gratiano wins her companion Nerissa. But their happiness is interrupted by the news that Antonio's enterprises have failed and Shylock is determined to exact his bond. Portia and Nerissa withdraw, ostensibly to go to a monastery, leaving Lorenzo and Jessica at Belmont. Instead they follow Bassanio and Gratiano to Venice.

At the court where Shylock's claim is tested the Duke cannot persuade him to relent. A lawyer is sent for but Portia and Nerissa, disguised as men, arrive in his place. Portia also tries to persuade Shylock to show mercy. Again he refuses, and she has to award him his pound of flesh. Shylock is about to take it when Portia tells him that the bargain has to be honoured literally: he must take the exact weight, without any blood. He tries to withdraw, but she invokes a law against aliens who threaten the lives of Venetian citizens. He is required to give Lorenzo and Jessica half his present wealth, to bequeath them his estate and to become a Christian.

Portia refuses to accept any fee from Bassanio but insists on taking his engagement ring. Nerissa follows suit with Gratiano. When the two women return to Belmont, they quarrel with their husbands for the apparent betrayal. Portia reveals the disguise, and they are all reconciled. She gives to Antonio a letter telling him he is rich again, three of his ships having arrived safely, and to Lorenzo Shylock's deed of gift.

SOURCES

Marlowe's *The Jew of Malta*, written around 1589–90 and revived in 1594 and 1596, was probably the main stimulus to the play. Its elements have a long history in folklore. The version of the bond story most likely to have been used by Shakespeare is Ser Giovanni Fiorentino's in *Il Pecorone* (1558). The closest version of the casket story is in the medieval *Gesta Romanorum* as translated in 1577. Jessica's elopement with Lorenzo probably comes from a story in the fifteenth-century *Novellini* of Masuccio. There may have been an intermediate source play called *The Jew*, now lost.

PART ONE: TEXT

1 INTRODUCTION

When is a text not a text? One of the answers to this question is: when the text is that of an Elizabethan play, like *The Merchant of Venice*, published after performance. For a number of reasons such a text lacks the integrity and stability which most people associate with the printed word. The most important is that Shakespeare did not write to be read but for performance. Publications of plays were not favoured by the groups of players who performed them and whose joint stock they were. Not until seven years after Shakespeare's death were his works collected in the Folio edition. Those of his plays, like *The Merchant of Venice*, which were published earlier in separate Quarto editions were probably brought out in response to demand and to inhibit pirated versions. While today, when a successful novel has been adapted to the screen, people speak of 'the film of the book', in Elizabethan times it was the other way round: 'the book of the play'.

One consequence of this is that some books of Shakespeare's plays, like *Hamlet*, *Othello* and *King Lear*, apparently record different performances from those recorded in the Folio. The texts had changed as a result of production. Differences between the earlier and later versions of *The Merchant of Venice* are relatively small – though it is only recently that two characters, Salerio and Solanio, have been distinguished from the three characters of earlier editions. Nevertheless, the fact of change highlights the provisional nature of Shakespearean texts, and points up limitations in the comparison often drawn between them and musical scores. Like a musical score a play text can only become real and alive in performance. But a play when performed offers much more room for variety than a piece of music. Not only may various productions of the same play differ strikingly but even various performances of the same production. In the freedom of the Elizabethan theatre, when there was little time for group rehearsal and no director to coordinate, the variety would have been even greater.

Yet the tendency in most modern productions of Elizabethan drama is to assimilate and simplify. The texts we know as *Hamlet*, *Othello* and *King Lear* are actually composites, put together from those parts of the earliest editions considered most satisfactory. In the modern theatre directors often organise productions around governing concepts, and are usually taken to task if no clear, unambiguous idea of the play emerges. Modern criticism has been dominated by a search for unified, determining interpretations, and this has taken several forms. Among them is source study. Often valuable in showing the nature and range of cultural influence, this much more frequently shows how a great play rewrites, refuses to be tied to, its material. Study of Elizabethan stage and literary conventions can also produce results which are double-edged. Research into the acting of Jewish parts in other Elizabethan plays cannot determine how Shylock was performed, for writers bend and question conventions as well as follow them. Equally, to demonstrate structural similarities between plots and character types is to go only so far. There may be worlds of difference in tone and quality when it comes to performance. Most of all, modern criticism has been dominated by a search for themes. A thematic overview comfortingly reduces complexity, and usually offers moral justification – for instance, in *The Merchant of Venice*, the superiority of Mercy to Justice. But if the text itself is unstable there is no lock for even the most ingenious thematic key.

In some ways Shakespeare's comedies seem designed to baffle those who try to pluck out the heart of their mystery. All have plots of staggering implausibility, and in *The Merchant of Venice* Shakespeare seems to have gone out of his way to heighten this. For example, there is Portia's amazing news at the end of the play that three of Antonio's ships have 'richly come to harbour' [v i 277]. Yet the figures who people the plays, though they often speak in verse, set up an equally staggering impression of human behaviour – an impression which is not only consistently credible but can become overwhelmingly powerful. As John Wilders expressed the paradox, in Shakespeare's comedies ' "real" people are caught up in "unreal" situations' (*Shakespeare, The Merchant of Venice: A Casebook*, 1969, p. 15). The result is very different from the realist or naturalist convention normal in much modern theatre, television and film. It is one of extraordinary creative freedom on Shakespeare's part, which ought to be honoured by those who produce and write about his work.

One reason why it is difficult to honour such freedom, and why it is difficult to speak of any text as stable and authoritative, has to do with how people read and perceive. Witnessing, judging and knowing depend on habits of perception by which information can be organised and absorbed. For this reason there is an important sense in which each reader reads not only a text but himself or herself, his or her particular set of cultural assumptions. For instance, most actors who have played Shylock have played him with an accent. Yet, though Shakespeare has given Shylock his own kind of language, distinguishing him from the other characters, there is no direct evidence of an accent in the text – as there is, for instance, with Fluellen the Welshman and others in *Henry V*, or with Edgar when he adopts a country accent in *King Lear*. The word 'moneys', sometimes thought to indicate Jewish pronunciation, used to be an orthodox plural and occurs elsewhere in Shakespeare. Again, productions have often distinguished Shylock by special costume but the basis for doing so is slight. Shylock's phrase 'Jewish gaberdine' [i iii 109] refers to no known garment and probably means an ordinary cloak. Similarly, only sources external to the play indicate that Venetian Jews were required to advertise their race with a red or yellow hat. Instead Portia's first question when she enters the court, 'Which is the merchant here? and which the Jew?' [iv i 171], suggests that there is no obvious difference in appearance between Antonio and Shylock. I quote the line as it appears in the Quarto and Folio texts. Most modern editions, like the Penguin, obscure the point by starting a new sentence at 'and', which slows the line down. These examples show how easy it is to assume details for which there is no explicit and little implicit textual authority, though in both cases they would strongly influence a production.

Nevertheless, in the examples just discussed the words of Shakespeare's playbook provide firm if not quite conclusive evidence. Though clues to performance are often difficult to recognise and understand, they are there at all levels of the words and actions of the drama. Stylistically there is the diction, the figurative language, the handling of verse and prose – all elements in the verbal interplay between the characters and their communication with the audience. Dramatically there is the nature of what is shown on stage, whether as visual image, pattern of movement or interaction. At a further level is evidence of construction and organisation. This includes a scene's development and placing, the juxtaposition of a scene or speech with another and the repetition of leading motifs. These are the resources I shall try to explore in what follows. Although I have argued that Shakespeare's text is not a text in the usual sense, and cannot be taken for granted, this means that studying it closely and as far as possible without prejudice becomes all the more important.

2   VENICE AND BELMONT

The Merchant of Venice is built on a set of contrasts. As with the two history plays which Shakespeare probably wrote immediately after it, its structure is contrapuntal. In *Henry IV, Parts 1 and 2* the action alternates between king and rebels, court and tavern. In *The Merchant of Venice* the contrast is between Venice and Belmont, and it is less straightforward than it appears. Shakespeare's counterpoint does not alternate easy positives and negatives but forces harder questions. In *Henry IV, Part I* Hotspur ends the scene of the rebels' conspiracy with the word 'sport' [I iii 302]. Repeated in the next scene by Gadshill as he sets up the robbery in which Hal and his friends are to take part [II i 70], the word calls attention to the ironic parallel between two disorderly enterprises. This kind of linking, similarly prompted by verbal repetition, also occurs in *The Merchant*.

Shakespeare's use of counterpoint must have been stimulated by the fluidity of action on the stage for which he wrote. Unlike the theatre which developed in the later seventeenth century, the Elizabethan and Jacobean stage used little scenery and did not distinguish sharply between scenes. This made for effects of juxtaposition like those which modern films achieve by crosscutting from one sequence to another, supplying visual and thematic links. In literary criticism Venice and Belmont have often been presented as opposites: the city, dominated by business, the risks of trade and debt, versus the country with its freedom, grace and leisure (literally, Belmont means 'fine mountain'). Such a contrast is easily achieved with lavish scenery, as in many Victorian and earlier twentieth-century productions. It is much less likely with a stage practically bare of scenery; and the parallel between Portia's words and Antonio's at the beginning of the two opening scenes does not encourage it. Antonio is not sad because of his commercial risks, though Salerio and Solanio paint them feelingly. Portia is not happy despite the apparent advantages of being lady of Belmont.

Several dramatic points are implied by this opening parallel. First Portia, though heiress of Belmont, frets under her father's will which allows her no freedom to 'choose' or 'refuse' a husband [I ii 22]. There is nothing she can do about her condition but sit it out and hope for the best. Similarly Antonio can neither ease his melancholy nor explain it, at least to Salerio and Solanio, and it leads him to a problem like Portia's. Though the bond is in various ways unlike the device of the caskets, both are arbitrary and apparently irrational threats: one to life and the other – so it seems to Portia, despite Nerissa's assurances – to happiness. The fluidity of Elizabethan staging would have encouraged a third suggestion. Near the end of the first scene Bassanio speaks romantically to Antonio of his quest for a golden fleece [I i 161–76]. Portia, in the following scene, enduring the attentions of unwelcome suitors, shows what it is like to be the object of such a quest.

Similar questions are suggested by the opening dialogues. According to Harley Granville-Barker, a pioneer in understanding Shakespeare's stagecraft, one main function of the conversation which opens the play is 'to paint Venice' ('Shakespeare's Venice', *Casebook*, p. 70). The verse given to Salerio and Solanio is unusually rich and flamboyant, evoking the extravagant luxury associated with the city. Yet there is also another side to their fanciful wit, thrown into relief by the colourless verse and limp rhythms of Antonio's melancholy. The two differ from him not only in chattering cheerfully but in their frank, crass materialism. Solanio declares in his first words that if he were as rich a trader as Antonio his feelings would be mortgaged to his enterprises [i i 15–17]. Salerio adds the outrageous and utterly worldly conceit that, in Antonio's position, he would not be able to attend church without being reminded by the stonework of the rocks that threaten his ship. In this way the opening dialogue introduces not only Antonio's melancholy, which helps motivate his taking of the bond, but also a question of values. Salerio and Solanio, though trying to cheer up their friend, expose their own shallowness by assuming that his worry is commercial. His distress, despite his apparent security as a merchant, implies that the satisfactions of wealth have strict limits.

Shakespeare is invariably very careful to establish the social standing of his characters, and although the characters he presents in *The Merchant* are Venetian they correspond to social types in Elizabethan England. E. C. Pettet has pointed out how the opening scene distinguishes between different members of the wealthier classes: Antonio the merchant, and Bassanio, Gratiano and Lorenzo the extravagant young gentry ('*The Merchant of Venice* and The Problem of Usury', *Casebook*, pp. 104–5). Although Pettet does not mention them, Salerio and Solanio also appear to be merchants, if apparently less successful, for in his parting words Antonio supposes that their business calls them away [i i 63–4]. Such differences are important, for the first words of the newcomers suggest a different standard of values again. Bassanio begins with: 'Good signors both, when shall we laugh?' [66]; and Gratiano spends a long speech playing 'the fool' [79]. Yet in the uncomfortable interview which follows between Antonio and Bassanio it is emphasised that laughing and playing have their costs. Antonio's emotional disturbance contrasts both with the blithe materialism of his first companions on stage and with the devotion to pleasure of their successors.

Shakespeare marks the distinction in a way that, characteristically, not only produces comedy but highlights the feelings of the person who is its object. The sequence involving Gratiano exploits a stock comic gambit, the interrupted departure. Lorenzo's first words tactfully indicate that Antonio is to be left alone with his friend. Bassanio's reply is a half line [I i 72], which usually indicates a pause. Here, this suggests that Lorenzo and Gratiano turn to leave – only for the latter to wreck his companion's courtesy and to comment with gross insensitivity on Antonio's unhealthy looks. Gratiano is wincingly and lengthily wrong about the cause of Antonio's depression, and his speeches call for two or even three further postponements to his exit – which Antonio must now heartily wish [100–1, 107, 111]. The effect is both comic and suggestive of the frivolous, insensitive side of Venice. No wonder Antonio responds to Gratiano's tasteless parting couplet with apparent irritation, even incoherence (both Quarto and Folio texts read 'It is that any thing now' [I i 113]).

The sequence between Antonio and Bassanio both helps to explain Antonio's sadness and develops the questions about values raised previously. Bassanio's expensive leisure has led to debts in money and love [131]; he proposes to repay Antonio's money through the love of Portia. The dialogue points up the resulting tensions. Alone with his friend, Bassanio shifts into casual prose, half-apologising light-heartedly for Gratiano. But for Antonio the issue between them is so important that it has to be faced directly. He immediately restores the more serious, formal medium of verse. Later, offering all his credit to Bassanio, he will abandon the formal 'you' for the intimate 'thou' [177, 182]. Bassanio's elaborate account of his predicament shows embarrassment, cast in relief by the increasing urgency of Antonio's appeals to say what he means. Bassanio speaks much more confidently in explaining his plan to go to Belmont, but even this raises further doubts. When he describes Portia it is ambiguous whether he places her attractions deliberately in ascending order of importance, or whether he corrects himself as he goes along:

> In Belmont is a lady richly left,
> And she is fair, and, fairer than that word,
> Of wondrous virtues. [161–3]

Portia's 'worth' [167] may be either moral or financial, or both, and there is a similar ambiguity about what kind of 'thrift' [175] Bassanio anticipates. Sometimes it is argued that such questions are modern subtleties which would not have troubled Elizabethans. But the dramatic context seems to make them inescapable. Not only is Bassanio asking for a loan in the hope of realising a further speculation, but, as I have tried to show, the respective values of money, pleasure and love are set at issue by the whole opening scene.

Just as the romantic appeal of Bassanio's quest is complicated by practical needs and motives, so Portia is no fairy-tale heiress. She begins by protesting at her lack of freedom to choose a husband and, understandably, not all the wit she displays behind her suitors' backs is tolerant. In depreciating them she introduces another contrast which is to gain importance. Often taken for granted in the theatre as a comic set piece, her mockery both betrays an edge of malice and sets up an opposition between insiders and outsiders which is to appear in a different way with Shylock. All the suitors Portia satirises are foreign, and it is their foreignness which is the joke: Neapolitans were known for their horsemanship, Frenchmen for courtesy, Germans for drunkenness. The point should not be pressed too hard, for the tone of the satire is fairly light. Portia acknowledges that 'it is a sin to be a mocker' [I ii 54], and even turns her jest against the audience when she describes the Englishman and his Scottish neighbour. Yet there is an underlying link with hostility to Shylock as an outsider. This is confirmed at the end of the scene by Portia's response to the Prince of Morocco's coming arrival: 'If he have the condition of a saint and the complexion of a devil, I had rather he should shrive me than wive me' [123–5]. Portia's gibe is aimed at Morocco's dark skin – like devils, associated at this period with hellfire. Later, on his entrance, Morocco's first words are: 'Mislike me not for my complexion' [II i 1], and Portia assures him that he stands 'as fair/As any comer' she has seen [20–2]. In one sense this is true, though again Morocco is excluded from the irony, for Nerissa and the audience know what Portia thinks of the suitors who have already come and gone. But 'fair' does not only mean 'fairly' or 'well', and the position of the word at the end of a run-on line emphasises its importance. As it will later in the play, the word also carries the meaning of 'fair skin'. Portia states her real attitude to Morocco when he has chosen unsuccessfully: 'Let all of his complexion choose me so' [II vii 79]. The contradiction between Portia's declared and her actual feelings raises the question whether she deserves sympathy for her invidious position or disapproval for her prejudice and insincerity. This is not the only occasion in the play when alternative responses are possible according to the nature of the audience – or perhaps a divided response.

3   THE CASKET SCENES

As the play progresses the contrasts with which it opened often seem, in much the same way, to become contradictions. The casket scenes provide a central example. At first sight the moral of the caskets is the difference between appearance and reality. According to traditional Christian teaching, gold and silver are things of this world and end there. The former is certainly desired by many men, as the casket's inscription declares, but the skull inside mocks worldly goods and desires. The latter carries a similar lesson, with the further twist that only a fool thinks he deserves well. Lead seems to fit the same message: appearances are deceptive, so a humble outside may mask a rich prize. In the event, however, such riddles do not quite work. If Morocco chooses wrongly because he infers a rich inside from a rich outside, Portia is wrong to judge him by 'the complexion of a devil' even though he may have 'the condition of a saint' [I ii 123–4]. If Bassanio chooses rightly because he refuses to be taken in by attractive appearances, this seems inconsistent with the fact that, as he has already said, not the least of Portia's attractions are her money and her beauty. Besides, Bassanio does not, according to the inscription on the lead casket, 'give and hazard all he hath' in any way that can be distinguished from the different choices of Morocco and Arragon. Portia uses the same word, 'hazard', to each of them [II i 45, II ix 18, III ii 2], for all have to risk perpetual celibacy if they fail. And what Bassanio has is at Antonio's hazard, courtesy of Shylock.

At this point, as elsewhere in *The Merchant of Venice*, it becomes necessary to consider whether the play exposes such contradictions or such contradictions expose the play. One possible way of resolving the question is to determine how an audience might respond to the various suitors. Morocco is 'a tawny Moor all in white' according to the stage direction, which is probably Shakespeare's [II i 0]. His train sounds equally impressive and his words are heroic both in form and content, unlike those of any other character in the play. He does not seem set up as a comic figure in any obvious sense. Although it would have been easy to show him reaching the wrong choice for foolish reasons, his speech not only shows a plausible process of deliberation but has its own logic. Rather than comic, Morocco's appeal is exotic. But by the same token he is not for Portia. One reason why his speech is not simply sent up is so that the audience may feel there is some danger he might choose rightly. Portia has already been shown fretting under the casket 'lottery' (both her own word [II i 15] and Nerissa's [I ii 27]), and objecting to the risk of a black husband. Her reason for objecting is implied in a pair of words whose double meanings resonate, as already suggested, elsewhere in the play. One of them, 'fair', occurs three times at the start of Bassanio's first description of Portia [I i 162–4] and three times in Morocco's casket speech [II vii 19–47]. This gives an edge to her use of the word in II i 20, discussed above, in reply to Morocco's 'fairest' in line 4 of the same scene. The other, more complex word is 'gentle'. When Morocco calls Portia 'my gentle queen' [II i 12], he means both that she is well born and that she has mild and tender manners to match. When, after he leaves in failure, she says: 'A gentle riddance' [II vii 78], she means more than 'good riddance' because she is playing on another, related word, 'gentile' – which means 'heathen'. Morocco is not a suitable husband because he is of the wrong race.

For another reason the Spaniard Arragon is no more suitable. No modern audience can respond as an Elizabethan audience would have responded to a representative of the country which had recently tried to invade its own. It is difficult here to avoid the impression that Shakespeare gratifies contemporary prejudice. Arragon with his supercilious self-importance is absurd in a way Morocco is not. Yet, again, even Arragon's speech does not simply evoke laughs. He easily avoids Morocco's mistake though he passes over the lead casket even more rapidly; and he speaks the truth in his words on 'undeservèd dignity' [ii ix 37–49] though he fails to apply it to himself. The point is again to keep up dramatic suspense, as is suggested by the pause at the end of his speech to which Portia's comment draws attention: 'Too long a pause for that which you find there' [53]. Portia's words show her relief, not only here but in the sharp put-down which follows in lines 61–2 and the contempt she vents on his departure ('O these deliberate fools!' [80]).

If Morocco and Arragon are set up, with more or less dramatic subtlety, as fall guys in the casket game, the question arises whether Bassanio does not get too easy a task. A line of critics stretching from the nineteenth century to the present has argued that he does, even to the point of being prompted by Portia in choosing correctly. The case rests mainly on the importance of the song, with which none of the other choosers are favoured. Its theme of misleading fancy, born of appearances, is relevant to Bassanio's choice, three of its lines end in sounds which rhyme with 'lead', and Bassanio's first words afterwards suggest a continuation of thoughts which the song may have hinted ('So may the outward shows be least themselves' [iii ii 73]). Yet Portia not only says she will not break her oath by telling him the right choice, but shows great concern in case he chooses wrongly; and on stage it is difficult to convey any prompting without further contrivance than the words offer. What seems more likely is that the audience is teased with the possibility that Portia may reveal the riddle. She displays her feelings for Bassanio all too plainly – Freud himself commented on what is now called a Freudian slip in the words: 'One half of me is yours, the other half yours,/Mine own I would say' [16–17] (*Introductory Lectures on Psychoanalysis* [Pelican Books, 1974], pp. 63–5). The dialogue which follows may be played with a subtext in which Bassanio tries delicately to draw out a hint and Portia just holds off, but it leads into a sustained passage of rich, extravagant poetry surrounding the choice and its result. The lavish verse and figurative language seem to celebrate a fairy-tale logic allowing a mutually happy ending.

Yet the logic of the casket scenes should not go unquestioned. In them, according to James Smith, 'the confusions of the crossword puzzle are multiplied by those of the brantub' (*Shakespearian and other essays*, 1974, p. 50). Smith argues that the speech in which Bassanio chooses is a tissue of commonplaces, that he wins by luck, and that this is plausible and human. It is debatable whether this could be conveyed in performance without cutting the speech heavily. The lines are in the same high-flown idiom as the speeches given by Portia immediately before and by Bassanio immediately afterwards. Perhaps more revealing is the contrast implied between what is heard and what is seen on stage. Bassanio speaks wisely of deceiving appearances. But he himself must be richly dressed: he has pleaded with Antonio for the 'means' to rival Portia's other suitors, and he has fitted Lancelot out very quickly with an elaborate livery. Dramatically the sequence is ambiguous. It is difficult to be sure whether the ironies work against the play or against Bassanio.

Less equivocal is a train of contrasts which unfolds directly after Bassanio's success. First, Bassanio shifts in a single speech from hyperbolic euphoria, in which he spends twelve lines praising Portia's picture before addressing the lady [114–26], to language which discloses her other attractions. As John Russell Brown has noted of line 140, 'To "come by note" meant to present one's bill or I.O.U.; Bassanio has "ventured" all and can now claim his "fortune"' ('Love's Wealth and the Judgement of *The Merchant of Venice*', *Casebook*, p. 166). Brown interprets the metaphor positively, in harmony with his view that the play sets 'love's usury' against the other kind practised by Shylock. But the persistence of language from law and accounting which he notes – such as Bassanio's 'Until confirmed, signed, ratified by you' [148] – recalls the conflict of values set up at the beginning of the play. Both Bassanio's and Portia's words pay witness to the fact that the marriage is a contract as well as a sacrament. Again, the 'unreal' situation John Wilders describes as characteristic of Shakespearean comedy gives way to a 'real' response.

The most obvious example of this in the same scene is that news of Antonio's arrest arrives at the height of the couple's happiness. In the play's probable main source, *Il Pecorone*, the hero forgets his benefactor until chance jogs his memory. Shakespeare allows Bassanio only the briefest satisfaction before reminding him what his venture may cost. The third corrective to easy romance concerns the change in Portia's position. Giving Bassanio her ring, she says:

> But now I was the lord
> Of this fair mansion, master of my servants,
> Queen o'er myself; and even now, but now,
> This house, these servants, and this same myself
> Are yours, my lord's. [167–71]

She gets a surprise when a few minutes later, Bassanio acts as if he is lord of the house already in welcoming his Venetian friends. Although Bassanio quickly draws back to apologise – itself a sign of how Portia may have reacted – some discomfort remains. Portia's line, 'They are entirely welcome' [225], is a short one, suggesting an embarrassed pause; and, as Ralph Berry suggests, if she meant it she would say 'You' and not 'They' (*Shakespeare and the Awareness of the Audience*, 1985, p. 56). The point is that she has escaped from her father's will only to give herself to a husband's. She must make what use she can of Bassanio's indebtedness, revealed at the most uncomfortable moment, to redress the balance.

The casket scenes develop a drama much more alive to its possible human implications than the framework of romantic comedy suggests. That drama is generated by two tensions introduced earlier in the play, involving a conflict of values between love and money and one of wills between woman and men. The quality of the comedy is unusual, stemming as it so often does from embarrassment, and it points to the critical, thoughtful nature of the play. Shakespeare's scepticism may go so far as to question Bassanio's claim to Portia. Yet the question remains whether Morocco's exclusion early in the play is in keeping with Shylock's later.

4   THE PROBLEM OF SHYLOCK

There are two main reasons why Shylock is a problem. One lies in the history of the Jews. Dispossessed from their homeland and scattered among other nations, victims of all forms of oppression to the dreadful extremes of pogrom and holocaust, their story should permanently warn against the appalling dangers of all racial prejudice. Under the Nazi régime, within the last 50 years, *The Merchant of Venice* was produced to incite racial hatred. If in any way the play encourages prejudice, those taking part in producing or discussing it carry heavy responsibility.

The second reason why Shylock is a problem lies in the nature of his role. There is no doubt that this is based on anti-Semitic stereotypes, and for that a kind of limited liability is sometimes claimed. There were so few Jews in Elizabethan England that Shakespeare is unlikely to have known any; nor could he have known what would happen subsequently to Shylock's race. But it is no good arguing that the play is a victim of history. In its own way it is implicated in that history if it fosters anti-Semitism. What is the evidence that the play defines Shylock both as a villain and, in the terms of its period, as typically Jewish?

To begin with the first question, Shylock hates Antonio and says so unequivocally in a long aside early in his first scene [I iii 38–49]. This is all the more telling because on the Elizabethan stage it would practically have been a soliloquy. Second, the usury practised by Shylock was seen by contemporaries as evil. John Russell Brown quotes from several Elizabethan tracts to show this (Arden edition, 1961, pp. xliv and 24–6). Similarly, W. Moelwyn Merchant notes the comments of the Bishops' Bible on the passage which Shylock applies to defend usury (New Penguin edition, pp. 174–5). In this light Antonio's response, 'The devil can cite Scripture for his purpose . . . O what a goodly outside falsehood hath!' [I iii 95–9], is no more than the truth. Third, Shylock denies natural human feelings. Not only do Jessica and Lancelot leave him, but, as John Russell Brown observes, 'nowhere in the play does Shylock show any tenderness towards his daughter'

(Arden edition, p. xli). His mingled lament for daughter and ducats is a case in point, especially the terrible curse: 'I would my daughter were dead at my foot, and the jewels in her ear! Would she were hearsed at my foot, and the ducats in her coffin!' [III i 80–2]. Shakespeare chose not to present Shylock's first grief directly but through Salerio and Solanio's mockery. The effect may be to devalue the impact of his suffering in III i. Then the same two not only give news of Antonio's losses but honour his kindness and generosity [II viii 35–53].

The later part of the play seems to strengthen these three main charges. If Shylock affirms his essential humanity when he asks 'Hath not a Jew eyes?' [III i 53], he affirms it through an appeal to the wish for revenge – a lowest common denominator between Jew and Christian. Yet the play seems to disable the suggestion that he becomes determined on revenge only after his daughter as well as his ducats are taken from him. Jessica herself gives the evidence:

> When I was with him, I have heard him swear
> To Tubal and to Chus, his countrymen,
> That he would rather have Antonio's flesh
> Than twenty times the value of the sum
> That he did owe him. [III ii 284–8]

The scene immediately following, in which Shylock harries the Jailer and Antonio expresses resignation [III iii], seems to have little other function than to emphasise his vengefulness. Yet he apparently keeps an instinct for profit. Having heard the news of Antonio's losses he declares: 'I will have the heart of him if he forfeit, for were he out of Venice I can make what merchandise I will' [III i 116–18]. Later, in the trial scene, he will be prepared to bargain for his claim against Antonio once he has to surrender the pound of flesh. Most of all, however, it seems impossible to get round the sheer, stark horror of what he proposes. As Ann Pasternak Slater has remarked, Shylock in the court scene is made to evoke the allegorical figure of Justice, 'knife and scales in either hand', but justice totally without mercy (*Shakespeare the Director* [Brighton, 1982], p. 177). He whets the knife on his shoe, shows no compunction at the danger of Antonio bleeding to death, and takes his deeds on his head in words which may echo those of the Jews who crucified Christ

(Penguin edition, p. 201). After Portia's verdict his earlier words of triumph are turned against him and he crumbles. He breaks the oath he had sworn, offers to take money instead and finally escapes by pleading sickness. Though Victorian productions, in a very different key, often ended with Shylock's defeat, the text all but ignores him after his final exit. Instead it gives the closing emphasis to Belmont.

If the play defines Shylock as a villain, a more controversial question is his race. John Barton has denied any link. Speaking for himself and the two actors he directed in the role, he says: 'We believe that [Shakespeare] shows Shylock as a bad Jew and a bad human being, but that this in itself does not make the play anti-Semitic' (*Playing Shakespeare*, 1984, p. 169). Barton suggests that Shylock is presented by the play as an individual, not as a representative of his race. He claims, for example, that the portrayal of neither Jessica nor Tubal is anti-Semitic, adding that one of Tubal's dramatic functions is to show 'how the Jewish community look at Shylock' (p. 178). Yet, as director of this judicious Tubal, Barton had him hand Shylock a bill for expenses. Arnold Wesker commented: 'The audience laughed again to be reminded that not only do Jews suck dry Christian blood, they suck each other's as well!' (*Guardian*, 29 August 1981). The play celebrates Antonio's generosity to his friends without acknowledging what Shakespeare may not have known, that Jews also took no interest from each other (though Shylock does say that Tubal will help him put up Antonio's loan [I iii 54–5]). It is less easy to free the play, or a production, of anti-Semitic attitudes than may seem.

Similarly, Barton's second example is disingenuous because Jessica's role is to become a converted Christian. When she claims that she is a daughter to Shylock's blood but not to his manners [II iii 18–19] there is every encouragement to agree with her, along with Lancelot [II ii 11–12, III v 5–10], Lorenzo [II iv 33–7]. Gratiano [II vi 51] and Salerio [III i 35–7]. Productions which give Shylock an accent usually take the hint by not giving Jessica one. Barton's 1981 production compromised with an accent that had faded by the end. Jessica's rebellion against her father is paralleled by Lancelot Gobbo's, and comics usually play with, not against, contemporary prejudices. The two characters are also the play's only speakers of soliloquies [II ii 1–28 (Lancelot), II iii 15–21 and II v 54–5 (Jessica)]. None of these invites the audience's disapproval.

Critics as well as directors sometimes deny a link between Shylock's villainy and his race. John Russell Brown has claimed that the play contains 'only two slurs on Jews in general' (Arden edition, p. xxxix). One comes from Lancelot Gobbo, 'My master's a very Jew' [II ii 97], the other from Antonio who says that there is no softening Shylock's 'Jewish heart' [IV i 80]. Yet these slurs declare respectively the twin stereotypes of anti-Semitism, miserly greed and evil malice. They are echoed by another example which Brown seems to have missed despite his own footnote, Lancelot's 'I am a Jew if I serve the Jew any longer' [II ii 104] ('a type of heartlessness', p. 41). Further, Brown's qualification ('only') forgets the cumulative effect of a word repeated so often in the play. The other characters refer to Shylock by the term 'Jew' much more often than by his name, and so do many of the stage directions, which are probably Shakespeare's own. Those who write on the play have often followed suit, and sometimes still do so – like Declan Kiberd in his student guide (York Notes, 1981).

Alan C. Dessen has proposed a way of understanding Shylock's Jewishness in its dramatic and historical context. In his article 'The Elizabethan Stage Jew and Christian Example' he discusses three Elizabethan plays which use the figure of a Jew as a moral type in order to catch Christian consciences (*Modern Language Quarterly 35*, 1974, pp. 231–45). One of these plays, Marlowe's *The Jew of Malta* (1589–90) with its outrageous hero, Barabas, unmistakably stimulated *The Merchant of Venice*. In Dessen's argument Shylock, like Barabas, is both villain and Jewish stereotype but his chief dramatic function is not anti-Semitic. Instead what he says and does as stage Jew rebukes the attitudes and behaviour of false Christians. On this view Shylock's key line is: 'The villainy you teach me I will execute, and it shall go hard but I will better the instruction' [III i 65–6]. Dessen argues that the present meaning of Shylock is anti-Semitic in a way it could not have been for the play's first audiences. He puts his reading forward as a way of saving the play from implications it cannot now escape.

Dessen opens the way to a better understanding of Shylock's role, but his argument needs qualification. First, as he himself admits, rescuing the play through literary history does not help it on the stage today. A modern audience cannot be equipped with Elizabethan ways of seeing. Second, there are important differences as well as similarities between Shylock and Marlowe's Barabas. The latter fits Dessen's case very well, but compared with Shylock he is a figure in a moral pantomime. Barabas is the larger-than-life hero of a satirical cartoon but Shylock has the human dimensions suggested, piercingly, by his lament for the loss of his ring: 'I had it of Leah when I was a bachelor' [III i 111–12].

There is some curious bibliographical evidence for the tension between Shylock's role as type and as individual. The original stage directions and speech prefixes refer to him sometimes by his name (normally abbreviated) and sometimes by the word 'Jew'. Both Quarto and Folio texts agree in every instance, with a few exceptions in the trial scene. John Dover Wilson tried to account for the discrepancy by supposing that the printing house was short of certain letters, but John Russell Brown rejects this (Arden edition, p. xvii). The setting up of the Quarto text by two different compositors (Arden, p. xiii) offers no better explanation. Instead it seems likely that the variations come from Shakespeare's manuscript, some form of which the compositors are thought to have used. Although the evidence is difficult to interpret, it seems plausible that Shakespeare thought of Shylock both in generic terms and as an individual, much as he thought of Lancelot Gobbo who is also referred to both by name and role ('Clown'). Even more interesting is the possibility that some of the changes correspond with shifts in the way the character is presented. Examples where the speech prefixes define Shylock as 'Jew' include the important aside in his first scene and the two speeches that precede it [I iii 28, 31, 38]; the sequence in which he harries Antonio and the Jailer [III iii 1–17]; and the height of his apparent triumph in the trial scene [IV i 247–301]. Examples with Shylock's own name are the whole of his first scene except for the three speeches noted; the whole of the scene at his home except for the first stage direction and speech prefix [II v]; the whole of III i where his anger and grief explode;

and for parts of the trial scene including all his speeches after
Portia has defeated him [ɪv i 333ff.]. In general, Shylock's
behaviour in the first set of examples fits the stereotypes; in the
second set it goes beyond them.

The third qualification to Dessen's argument is that, as
numerous performances have shown, the part like the play is
extraordinarily rich. No evidence exists of how Shylock was
acted on the Elizabethan stage. We should beware of
attributing to Shakespeare and his audiences the cruelty of our
own century. Fundamentally drama shows human interaction.
That interaction gains power and conviction by presenting a
variety of perspectives. Shakespeare is a great dramatist by
virtue of his ability to suggest the many-sidedness of people and
events. Although he drew on stereotypes in creating Shylock, it
does not follow that he limited himself to them. Yet this is what
is often assumed. Soon after his first entry Shylock lays down
the terms of his dealings with Bassanio: 'I will buy with you, sell
with you, talk with you, walk with you, and so following; but I
will not eat with you, drink with you, nor pray with you'
[ɪ iii 33–5]. More than one critic has suggested that this speech
is an aside – John Russell Brown quotes the New Cambridge
editor as commenting: 'It would be unlike the Jew to reveal his
hate openly at this stage' (Arden edition, p. 23). The
suggestion illustrates, however, not only how one-sided much
discussion of Shylock has been but how lacking in dramatic
awareness. In context Shylock's speech much more plausibly
mocks Bassanio's hypocrisy in offering social pleasantries to
one whom he consults only because he needs money.

The dramatic action Shakespeare provides bristles with
challenges like this. In Chapter 2 I suggested that the scenes
alternating between Venice and Belmont do not necessarily
contrast the real, consequential world of the city with a world of
love and romance. Just as, in the first two scenes, Portia's
sadness is juxtaposed with Antonio's and linked in turn to the
quest described by Bassanio, so there is a link between the end
of the second scene and the start of the third when Shylock first
enters. Again the link would have been emphasised by the
fluidity of Elizabethan staging. Portia's last words are: 'Whiles
we shut the gate upon one wooer, another knocks at the door'
[ɪ ii 126–7]. The next scene begins with another wooer,

Bassanio, applying to Shylock for the money he needs in his courtship.

Similarly, if Bassanio is exposed by the beginning of ı iii, ridiculously using the language of courtesy to a man he would otherwise avoid, Antonio is exposed by what follows. On his entry the scene switches from prose to verse, indicating a change of tone, and Bassanio's short first line, 'This is Signor Antonio' [37], suggests a pause. That pause gives Shylock the opportunity to move downstage for his aside. But the aside is dramatically stronger if it is motivated, and the most likely motive is that Antonio ignores Shylock. This is consistent both with Antonio's hatred, described by Shylock later in the scene, and with the fact that Bassanio must tell his friend that Shylock is prepared to lend the money. Further, Shylock's aside is surprisingly long in that its second two sentences merely repeat and amplify the first two. It is plausible that at the end of line 44, 'I will feed fat the ancient grudge I bear him', he looks to the other two, finds them still talking, and continues his aside until Bassanio rudely calls to him, breaking his speech at a half line. Then he can cover up by pretending surprise at seeing Antonio and by welcoming him with studied over-politeness. Antonio may himself be surprised and displeased by the lender Bassanio has found him, and the following encounter shows his hatred all too plainly. His request for the money is grudging and peremptory, his other speeches clipped and abrupt. In the 'Laban' speech [ı iii 73–87] Shakespeare gave Shylock the chance to justify usury as an insider to Jewish culture might have understood it. But Antonio rejects the explanation scornfully and then, interrupting, tells Bassanio before Shylock's face what he thinks of it. This is the kind of treatment which Shylock goes on to deprecate. It is further confirmed by Antonio's reply, adding more insult by dropping the formal 'you' for the familiar 'thou' [127–34].

Such examples fit Dessen's view of Shylock as a Jew who shows up bad Christian example. Less consistent with such a view is Shylock's humour. This is not always noticed, so often has he been presented as speaking and acting with teeth-clenched malignity. Here he laughs out loud when Bassanio bridles at the word 'good', puns on the word 'pirates', and even mocks the priggish formality of Bassanio's speech in repeating the word 'assured' [27–9]. Later in the scene he humorously enjoys his account of 'the work of generation' between Jacob's 'woolly breeders' [79–80], and jokes at his own reputed hunger for profit when he declares: 'A pound of man's flesh taken from a man/Is not so estimable, profitable neither/As flesh of muttons, beefs, or goats' [162–4]. Most of all, his humour allows him to control the dialogue while Antonio loses his temper. To the other's ungraciousness in expecting a loan while disapproving of usury he replies by defending the taking of interest. When Antonio questions the analogy between increase of stock and increase of money, Shylock turns the tables wittily: 'I cannot tell, I make it breed as fast' [93]. The great speech in which he demonstrates the hypocrisy and injustice of Antonio's behaviour is an object lesson in irony [I iii 103–26]. Antonio's angry response betrays how little he understands.

Shylock's first scene is not alone in showing his discomfiting wit. In his last scene it is even sharper. His indictment of Venetian hypocrisy for owning slaves but not allowing him his legal property [IV i 89–103] is as unanswerable as his protest to Antonio in I iii. Beyond this is the comic, outrageous defiance of his 'humour' or arbitrary will [IV i 40–62]. Shylock scandalises the solemnity of the court with his homespun, bizarre examples – especially the effect of bagpipes on an over-sensitive bladder. This is the raw, rueful irony of the outsider, his weapon against humiliations he cannot help noticing because his nose is rubbed in them so often. Later Shylock goes as far as the black, bitter humour of sharpening his knife on his sole, and pretending to scan the bond for a reference to a surgeon [IV i 259].

Shylock resembles other subversive figures in Shakespeare who develop a disturbing rapport with their audiences: Richard III, Falstaff, Iago, Edmund in *King Lear*. His unrespectable wit goes back to that of their common literary ancestor, the Vice of the Morality plays, and like theirs it upsets conventional perceptions. Yet there are important distinctions between each of these roles, and none is simply that of moral agent provocateur. One sign of this with Shylock is that his behaviour, unlike that of Marlowe's Barabas, keeps changing. He does not act in private as in public. Confident in his first scene and never at a loss, he is shown by the scene in his own home [II v] in a wholly different light. This is the Jew as Puritan, a jealous, vulnerable householder and father. Second, the play demonstrates not only his anger but his grief. If there is any inclination to laugh at this, more than once it seems designed to wipe any smile off the audience's face. Salerio and Solanio mock Shylock's lament for daughter and ducats only to remind themselves, chillingly, of the possible consequence: 'Let good Antonio look he keep his day,/Or he shall pay for this' [II viii 25–6]. Presented directly in the next scene but one, that grief and rage is anything but comic. Again, at the climax of the trial scene there is a comic moment – though characteristically uncomfortable – when Bassanio and Gratiano volunteer in the hearing of their wives to sacrifice them. Shylock's comment is again a bitter reminder of his own perspective and feelings:

> These be the Christian husbands! I have a daughter;
> Would any of the stock of Barabbas
> Had been her husband, rather than a Christian.   [IV i 292–4]

At a deeper level there is a string of puns on several words in the play including not only 'fair' and 'gentle', as mentioned in Chapter 3, but also that keyword of the tragedies, 'kind'. When Shylock begins to propose his bond he says, 'This is kind I offer' [I iii 139], and the word resonates through the rest of the scene, to be echoed at the end by Antonio with its counterpart: 'Hie thee, gentle Jew./The Hebrew will turn Christian; he grows kind' [174–5]. As modern editors point out, the word 'kind' meant not only 'benevolent' but 'natural', so in offering the bond Shylock counters what Antonio says is the usurer's ungenerosity. But the root sense of the word was 'related by kinship', and this is repeated in Antonio's paradox 'gentle Jew' – a paradox not only because Antonio thinks Jews are ungenerous, but because, as elsewhere, the adjective also evokes 'gentile'. What this wordplay may suggest is that the play's Christians have difficulty in seeing members of other racial groups as humane or human.

In this lie the remarkable contradictions of the trial scene. That is what it is, for although technically, as Patrick Stewart has argued, 'no one is on trial and there is no formal court'

(*Players of Shakespeare*, ed. Philip Brockbank, 1985, p. 24), in effect Shylock is both tried and sentenced. He is not only alone but the object of hostility from everyone on stage. The Duke describes him privately to Antonio as an 'inhuman wretch' [IV i 4], yet on his entry appeals to him in words he has just belied: 'We all expect a gentle answer, Jew' [34]. Later, despite Portia's assurance that 'the Venetian law/Cannot impugn you as you do proceed' [175–6], that law is to brand Shylock as what he has been to the Venetians all along, an 'alien' [346]. The point is unique to Shakespeare's version of the story, but its effect is not necessarily to emphasise, as John Russell Brown suggests, 'that Shylock is defeated on his own grounds of law and justice' (Arden edition, p. li). Rather it shows there is a different law, and 'justice', for the outsider.

Such problems come to a head in Shylock's sentence. One view, represented among others by Alan Dessen and the Penguin editor, W. Moelwyn Merchant, contrasts Shylock's own treatment with what he proposed for Antonio. According to Nevill Coghill's influential essay, it is the Old Law versus the New ('The Basis of Shakespearian Comedy', *Shakespeare Criticism 1935–1960*, ed. Anne Ridler [1963], pp. 201–27). In its own terms such a distinction is wholly valid. According to Venetian law half Shylock's goods are due to Antonio, the other half to the state, and his life lies at the Duke's discretion. In the event he is to escape with his life and half his goods on three conditions: he must become a Christian, Antonio must hold the other half of his goods in trust for Lorenzo, and he must leave all his property to Lorenzo and Jessica on his death. There is no denying that this is milder treatment than the law provides. What is often overlooked, however, is that both the 'justice' and 'mercy' are strictly Venetian. Shylock's treatment only appears merciful in contrast to the dire penalties with which he is threatened and in accordance with a Christian perspective. The Venetians may consider they are favouring a Jew by converting him. That is not how Shylock experiences it ('I pray you give me leave to go from hence,/I am not well' [IV i 392–3]), and he accepts the conditions only on pain of death. Similarly, the words with which Antonio shows 'mercy' suggest more of a desire to twist the knife by reminding Shylock of his losses: his goods are to go 'unto the gentleman/That lately stole his

daughter' [381–2]. In her most famous speech Portia defines
the quality of mercy as absolute. The mercy Shylock receives is
nothing if not relative, yet it is questioned only by Gratiano who
wishes it were still harsher.

If this understanding of the trial scene is acceptable, it
becomes possible to see Shylock's implacable insistence on his
bond in a different light. The issues are not the abstracts of
justice and mercy because these emerge as contingent. Instead
it is a scene concerned with power – a power held ultimately by
the Christian majority, but for a time by an outsider who tries,
on the basis of his apparent rights, to exact a terrible revenge on
those who injure and despise him. Shakespeare began with the
stereotypes of Jew and villain, which define the broad outlines
of Shylock's role. But developing that role brought out
awkward questions – not only legal and moral, but political and
human.

Among the qualities of great writing is its ability to stretch to
their limits the understandings conventional to its period.
Shakespeare wrote at a time of social and moral upheaval, in
which medieval notions of usury gave way to modern, and
traditional ideas of the human and political orders came into
question. He wrote in a form uniquely capable of exploring
conflict and contradiction. Like Marlowe's *Jew of Malta*, *The
Merchant of Venice* starts from anti-Semitic assumptions, but
whereas Marlowe satirised Christian example Shakespeare did
this and more. Shakespeare's play may be linked with the later
comedies *All's Well That Ends Well* and *Measure for Measure*. All
three stem from their particular historical period and show its
pressure. Yet all, through their richness in dramatic tension
and contradiction, are unusually open and many-sided. It is a
mistake, and a peculiarly modern one, to expect neat moral
attitudes and answers from plays which so test their audiences.

5   A 'PLAY UNPLEASANT'

Charged with such power to disturb, Shylock's story gives
every reason for borrowing Shaw's phrase, as W. H. Auden did,

and calling *The Merchant of Venice* one of Shakespeare's 'Plays Unpleasant' ('Brothers and Others', *Casebook*, p. 227). But if, as I have been arguing, Shylock must be understood in his dramatic context, it is equally important to recognise the other problems the play presents. These involve most of the characters, including Portia. For *The Merchant of Venice* also anticipates *Measure for Measure* and *All's Well That Ends Well* in raising questions about the role of women.

The problem of Portia is rooted in her subjection to male will and her need to overcome it. Her first main speech plays on the word: 'so is the will of a living daughter curbed by the will of a dead father' [i ii 23–4]. This is a double bond: the device of the caskets requires her to abide both by her father's will and its results. No wonder, lacking her own will, she gibes at her suitors behind their backs. After undergoing the dangers that the wrong man might win her, she bursts out in joy and relief when Bassanio chooses correctly. Immediately, though, another male-created constraint faces her in the shape of the bond. Again the problem is double, and it cannot be solved by money. There is Shylock's bond, to be exacted from Antonio. But, implicitly, Antonio has a bond as well. In his readiness to die for Bassanio he stakes an emotional claim as difficult in its way to repay as a pound of flesh. To remove these threats to her happiness with the husband she has only just married, Portia has to enter the world of men which has contrived them.

It is well known that until the Restoration in 1660 female parts in the theatre were normally played by boys or young men. What is not so well known is that Shakespeare was almost unique in exploiting what seems a natural twist to this convention, in that several heroines of his comedies, like Portia, adopt male disguise. In such cases a theatrical double-bluff operates: a male plays a female playing a male. This implies a special interest in gender roles and their complexities, one which goes beyond both theatrical convenience and narrative convention. Some of that interest is conveyed by the surprising glee with which Portia explains to Nerissa her plan to save Antonio:

> I'll hold thee any wager,
> When we are both accoutered like young men,

I'll prove the prettier fellow of the two,
And wear my dagger with the braver grace,
And speak between the change of man and boy
With a reed voice, and turn two mincing steps
Into a manly stride, and speak of frays
Like a fine bragging youth, and tell quaint lies,
How honourable ladies sought my love,
Which I denying, they fell sick and died –
I could not do withal.   [III iv 62–72]

The speech not only calls comic attention to the double-bluff I have mentioned. In context it suggests that the reason for Portia's glee, irrespective of the dangerous circumstances, is the enjoyment she promises herself in a male role, freed from Belmont.

Male disguise is fundamental to Portia's success in dealing with the threats to her happiness. First, she has to save Antonio in order both to discharge Bassanio's debt and to free him from misery at his friend's fate. Again emotional and financial realities are interwoven, as when Portia says: 'Since you are dear bought, I will love you dear' [III ii 313]. Then she must ensure that the friendship between Bassanio and Antonio does not threaten her marriage, as is only too likely in view of what Antonio undergoes for his friend. Of this she and the audience receive clear warning when, near the climax of the trial scene, Bassanio tells Antonio he would be prepared to sacrifice his wife to save him [IV i 279–84]. Only as a man can Portia enter the Duke's tribunal and give the judgement which will save Antonio. Only as a man can she take from Bassanio the ring with which she will ensure his future fidelity.

In the second part of the play Portia is as active and assertive as she was passive and subdued in the first. But having her will brings problems too. One of these occurs in the trial scene, where she refuses Shylock the mercy which she had previously asked for Antonio. The paradox is sometimes explained by arguing that Portia first gives Shylock every chance, but that he condemns himself by insisting on strict justice. According to Sinead Cusack, who played the role in John Barton's 1981 production, Portia is even more concerned to save Shylock than Antonio but he will not let her (*Players of Shakespeare*, p. 39).

However such a reading is inconsistent both with the terms of Portia's speech, in which mercy is absolute and unconditional, and with her refusal to intercede at the end. Her question 'What mercy can you render him?' [IV i 375] draws from Antonio provisos whose bitterness for Shylock I have already discussed. The speech on mercy is usually delivered in the theatre as a moving plea which embodies the qualities it describes. Yet it is very much a set piece in its careful, rhetorical construction, developing through nice antitheses to an impressively built climax. In context it is a public, forensic performance rather than a private appeal. Portia is laying down the moral law, and her tone is less that of compassionate persuasion than of the sermon or lecture. The reason for her insistence is not only to save Antonio but to safeguard her marriage. Yet she has no apparent reason for pursuing the case against Shylock to the point where it contradicts the high principles of which she has spoken. The irony is that, dressed as she is in male clothing, she shows some of the rigidity and oppression which the play associates with male will.

The trial scene does not provide the only example of Portia's strong-mindedness. In the play's closing sequence she puts Bassanio uncomfortably on the spot in asking for the ring he gave to his friend's saviour. Portia may not know that he gave the ring only at Antonio's urging, but she has to reclaim it in order to redress the balance of his loyalties. With a comic relentlessness she persists in her deception until Antonio makes a pledge to complement and redeem the one to Shylock:

> I dare be bound again,
> My soul upon the forfeit, that your lord
> Will never more break faith advisedly. [v i 251–3]

This is her cue to return to Bassanio the ring which symbolises their union, to reveal her part in the trial scene, and to reward the astonished Antonio with her news that three of his ships are 'richly come to harbour' [v i 277]. For her the ending is triumphant, yet it leaves other problems unresolved. The triumph is at Shylock's expense, and Antonio's. Questions also remain about some of those whom it apparently includes. Among these is Jessica, whose story both compares and contrasts with Portia's. She too begins the play in subjection to male will. Unlike Portia she rebels, but like her she gains freedom by dressing as a male. However the nature of this freedom is dubious. She robs her father as well as leaves him, and the extravagance reported by Tubal tells against her. Most of all, Jessica is not very welcome at Belmont. When she arrives there with Lorenzo and Salerio there is the embarrassing moment when Bassanio acts as master of the house too soon. Neither he nor Portia welcomes Jessica. It takes Gratiano, of all people, 17 lines after the entry, to notice her: 'Nerissa, cheer yond stranger; bid her welcome' [III ii 237]. In what follows Jessica has a single speech, in which she emphasises her father's hatred for Antonio [284–90]. This may be a sad attempt at affirming whose side she is on and so attracting the welcome and support she has not won. But Portia pointedly ignores her, turning to Bassanio: 'Is it your dear friend that is thus in trouble?' [291]. Similarly, Portia has very little to say to Jessica when they meet again in III iv and v i. She even has Nerissa deliver good news at the end – news first and foremost for Lorenzo: 'How now, Lorenzo?/My clerk hath some good comforts too for you' [v i 288–9]. Jessica's story suggests that it is not so easy to become 'a gentle and no Jew' [II vi 51]. It does not seem a coincidence that this phrase is later echoed by the Duke to her father: 'We all expect a gentle answer, Jew' [IV i 34]. The result is to complicate the relation between her story and Shylock's.

Two of the play's interludes involve Jessica, and both raise questions of tone. The first, in III v, allows for Portia and Nerissa's journey to Venice; the second, at the start of v i, for their return and change of costume. As usual Shakespeare turns narrative or theatrical necessity into dramatic opportunity. In the first sequence, which immediately precedes the trial scene, Lancelot jokes about Jessica's conversion. Her ingenuous replies suggest embarrassment, especially as she says nothing after her speech on Lorenzo's entry until, over 30 lines later, he asks: 'How cheer'st thou, Jessica?' [III v 65]. In the second sequence the talk is of legendary lovers. On the surface the mood is idyllic, but, as the Penguin editor notes (pp. 203–4), each example is ominous. Shakespeare was later to write the tragedy of Troilus and Cressida, he had already burlesqued that of Pyramus and Thisbe in *A Midsummer Night's Dream*, and in *The Merchant of Venice* there are several previous references to the story of Jason and Medea. For all the apparent playfulness there is little promise in these resonances – especially when Lorenzo puns on the word 'steal' (i.e. both 'escape' and 'rob' [v i 15]), and when Jessica repeats the word in questioning his fidelity: 'Stealing her soul with many vows of faith,/And ne'er a true one' [19–20]. The moment is ambiguous, like the speech in which Lorenzo first celebrates the music of the spheres and then calls attention to the fallen state of humanity which prevents hearing it [v i 54–65].

If the play's romance carries ominous overtones, its comedy is also uncomfortable. Lancelot's gentle baiting of the converted Jessica is not the only example. It has been suggested that the name 'Gobbo' may mean that both Lancelot and his father were played as hunchbacks (Penguin edition, p. 179). If this is so, it is of a piece with the sick humour of the sequence in which Lancelot tells his blind father he is dead [II ii 43–74]. Yet it would be wrong to assume that the effect would have been any funnier on the Elizabethan stage than today. As with Shylock, the dialogue argues differently. For Lancelot's practical joke misfires. Poignantly, his father is only too fully taken in, so that the emphasis falls on his blindness and not his openness to trickery: 'Alack, sir, I am sand-blind. I know you not' [II ii 68; I omit the Penguin edition's exclamation mark]. As elsewhere the play reminds its audiences of what they may be laughing at.

Gratiano is one of the main sources of this unsettling comedy. Crass, insensitive figures such as he are often humorous on stage. In the first scene the play shows both the comic and – to Antonio – the irritating side of his loudmouth prolixity, especially when he keeps promising but refusing to go. Here and elsewhere he has most of the play's bawdy jokes. Bassanio's request that he behave himself in Belmont [II ii 167–76] suggests, again, that the effect can be uncomfortable. An example occurs after his friend's betrothal to Nerissa. Bassanio politely says the right thing, 'Our feast shall be much honoured in your marriage' [III ii 212], only for Gratiano to joke obscenely about which couple will have the first son. The moment passes thanks to the greater embarrassment, when three other Venetians arrive, of Bassanio assuming prematurely the duties of host. But Portia later rebukes Gratiano ('Speak not so grossly' [v i 266]) for his crude question in the final scene about the apparent cuckolding.

It is in the trial scene that Gratiano disconcerts most. Shylock's most hostile and vocal opponent, his triumphant tauntings after Portia's victory may represent the mingled relief, exhilaration and rancour which those on stage (and in some audiences?) wish to express but cannot. Alternatively, his outbursts may be so obviously distasteful as to inhibit just such responses. It is absurd that he should exult, 'Now, infidel, I have you on the hip!' [IV i 331], when it is Portia who has defeated Shylock. Yet there is an ambiguity when the Duke follows Gratiano's most vindictive speech with the words: 'That thou shalt see the difference of our spirit,/I pardon thee thy life before thou ask it' [365–6]. The sentence Shylock receives is only less obviously cruel than the one Gratiano calls for. His crude brutality may be a better guide than it looks to the attitudes of those present. The last words of the play, spoken by Gratiano, also raise questions. Perhaps out of Portia's hearing, as the characters leave the stage, and despite her rebuke, he cracks another gross joke: 'Well, while I live I'll fear no other thing/So sore as keeping safe Nerissa's ring' [v i 306–7]. Not only is it strange that Gratiano should give the final speech – rather as if Sir Toby Belch were to speak last in *Twelfth Night*, or Lucio in *Measure for Measure*. This couplet, with its play on male and female sexual organs in the two rhyme words, is also an unusual note on which to end – especially in a scene which has invoked heavenly harmony.

The play's nominal hero is Antonio, and for different reasons his share in that harmony is equally doubtful. It is sometimes argued that Antonio's relation to Bassanio is homoerotic, and modern productions often bring this out in order to motivate his sad devotion. The play gives no explicit evidence on the matter – except that one element in the action is a trial of love between Antonio and Portia. At the beginning Antonio is prepared not only to let his friend go but to fund his wooing. Later he is prepared to die for him as the price. Yet it is as if, recognising he must lose Bassanio, he claims a kind of reward. It is difficult not to hear a reproach in his letter summoning

Bassanio from Belmont: 'all debts are cleared between you and I if I might but see you at my death. Notwithstanding, use your pleasure. If your love do not persuade you to come, let not my letter' [III ii 318–21]. Similarly in the trial scene he casts himself as a martyr for love, outbidding Portia:

> Commend me to your honourable wife,
> Tell her the process of Antonio's end,
> Say how I loved you, speak me fair in death,
> And when the tale is told, bid her be judge
> Whether Bassanio had not once a love.   [IV i 270–4]

The appeal verges on melodrama – and masochism. It is answered not only by Bassanio's empty boast that he 'would lose all' for Antonio [283], and by his and Gratiano's willingness to sacrifice their wives to save him. Sardonic comments from Portia and Nerissa follow, but then the tone shifts from uneasy comedy to the irony and pathos of Shylock's comment:

> These be the Christian husbands! I have a daughter;
> Would any of the stock of Barabbas
> Had been her husband, rather than a Christian.   [292–4]

This reverses the perspective to bring out the emptiness of each man's declaration – perhaps also Antonio's sentimentality. The other side of that sentimentality is hatred of Shylock. If Antonio shares his hatred with his friends, especially Gratiano, Salerio and Solanio, it still has the irrational violence of a man deeply frustrated and dissatisfied.

In the trial scene Portia defeats Antonio's claim against her husband as well as Shylock's against Antonio. In the final scene she afflicts him further with consolation. He takes comically doleful responsibility for the accusations about the rings: 'I am th'unhappy subject of these quarrels' [v i 238]. Portia then waits for him to guarantee Bassanio's future good behaviour before handing out forgiveness and good news. It is as if Shakespeare went out of his way to underline the absurdity of Antonio's last-minute luck – and of Portia knowing it. Well might he say 'I am dumb!' [279]. If Solanio is right in thinking that Antonio 'only loves the world' for Bassanio [II viii 50], it is difficult to believe his reply to Portia: 'Sweet lady, you have given me life and living' [v i 286]. Instead, his final position also strikes an uncertain note.

The play's last act is often seen either as an harmonious idyll or as an irrelevant indulgence. I have tried to suggest both that it completes the action and that it sustains some of the moral and dramatic tensions played on elsewhere. In Chapter 1 I argued that there is no such thing as a pure text. All texts are embedded in cultural and historical circumstance, and no readings can be innocent. But some readings are more guilty than others in distorting the evidence or presenting it selectively. It is often a mistake to smooth out apparent inconsistencies, for these may have dramatic point or call stock attitudes in question. The view of the play I have given emphasises its discords and contradictions. I believe this is consistent with what we know as the text, with social and dramatic history and with Shakespeare's practice in similar plays. It is a view which cannot help springing from my own attitudes and the place and time I inhabit, as well as from study and discussion. But it is better to acknowledge this than to pretend to a false objectivity. In the study of drama, comparison of different productions allows bias and dogma to be checked. That is partly the aim of what comes next. Not only are texts realised in performance. Often performance changes what was thought of as the text.

PART TWO: PERFORMANCE

6 INTRODUCTION: DESIGN AND STAGING

The five main productions I will discuss are as follows:

1. The National Theatre Production of 1970, directed by Jonathan Miller; Laurence Olivier as Shylock; Joan Plowright as Portia; Anthony Nicholls as Antonio; Jeremy Brett as Bassanio; designed by Julia Trevelyan Oman. Directed for television by John Sichel, 1973.

2. The RSC studio production of 1978, directed by John Barton; Patrick Stewart as Shylock; Marjorie Bland/Lisa Harrow as Portia; David Bradley as Antonio; John Nettles as Bassanio; designed by Christopher Morley.

3. The BBC-TV production of 1980, produced by Jonathan Miller; directed by Jack Gold; Warren Mitchell as Shylock; Gemma Jones as Portia; John Franklyn-Robbins as Antonio; John Nettles as Bassanio; designed by Oliver Bayldon.

4. The RSC main house production of 1981, directed by John Barton; David Suchet as Shylock; Sinead Cusack as Portia; Tom Wilkinson as Antonio; Jonathan Hyde as Bassanio; designed by Christopher Morley.

5. The RSC main house production of 1984, directed by John Caird; Ian McDiarmid as Shylock; Frances Tomelty as Portia; Christopher Ravenscroft as Antonio; Adam Bareham as Bassanio; designed by Ultz.

These productions have been chosen for the variety they offer not only in interpretation of the play and its characters but in the mode of production and design. One contrast is in the type of theatre and stage. While the National Theatre production of 1970 took place on the proscenium stage of the Old Vic, the 1978 RSC production was performed in the round in the bare studio conditions afforded by The Other Place at Stratford-upon-Avon. The combination of thrust and proscenium stage in the Royal Shakespeare Theatre provides a mean between these extremes, and this was the arena for the RSC productions of 1981 and 1984, though exploited very differently. A second obvious contrast is between stage productions and Jack Gold's television production for the BBC – supplemented by the television film made in 1973 of Jonathan Miller's National Theatre production. Further comparisons arise from two of the directors returning to the play: John Barton after three years and Jonathan Miller after ten years as producer of the BBC version.

I also have more specific reasons for choosing these productions. Three of them, Jonathan Miller's with the National Theatre and John Barton's pair with the RSC, were widely recognised as breaking new ground with the play. The BBC production raises different questions, designed as it is both to keep and to travel well through the resources of television and video. Finally, in John Caird's 1984 Stratford production I have included an example which illustrates some of the problems in staging the play today. I have chosen to discuss recent national productions in England because information is more easily available on them than on others. But *The Merchant of Venice* has long been international property, and performances in other countries, especially in Germany, Israel and America, also have much to contribute to understandings of the play.

I begin with differences in design and setting, not because I think these the most important but because they are the most immediately obvious and can help, or restrict, a production greatly. One of the main ways in which a director can seek to control a play is by setting it in a different time and place from what is stated or implied in the text. Recent productions of *The Merchant of Venice* have often done just that, including three of the five to be discussed.

The most controversial of these was Jonathan Miller's for the National Theatre in 1970. Michael Langham's production at Stratford in 1960 seems to have set off a rash of eighteenth-century settings. Repudiating these, Miller placed the play in the 1880s. Julia Trevelyan Oman's set used ingeniously the area provided by a proscenium stage. Its main location was St Mark's Square in Venice, complete with background steeples and colonnades. This opened out on one side to reveal Shylock's house, on the other Portia's; and gave way in Act IV to become the Duke's chamber. The set's chief impact, emphasised by costume and decoration, was one of luxurious materialism. This was a late Victorian Venice, swathed in the spoils and toils of capital.

For some reviewers the detail of Miller's set summoned up an array of allusions which extended from Disraeli to Oscar Wilde and Galsworthy's Forsytes. It emphasised that everyone was involved in money. Antonio was a successful but jaded businessman, Bassanio and his friends a younger generation bent on pleasure but dependent on a wealth they took for granted. Portia was an heiress whose home, richly and ornately furnished, was a monument to conspicuous consumption. Consequently a second effect was to demystify, even debunk, Belmont. Instead of exploiting the contrast between Venice and Belmont as so many previous productions had done, this one played it down. Belmont, it was suggested, was neither romantic nor mysterious, but the product of money too. Accordingly, although the country house trappings impressed as intended, the first two casket scenes were played for laughs. Morocco became a ludicrous minstrel figure with absurd accent and mannerisms, Arragon a senile dodderer whose comic business included taking six sugar lumps for his coffee, stirring it with the tongs and then putting them in his pocket, to be deftly retrieved by Nerissa. Miller even sent up part of Bassanio's scene by surprising him, and the audience, with the sudden arrival of two Victorian ladies to warble lushly the song on fancy. The effect was to remind the audience that the play was a comedy, but to confine the comedy to Belmont. Another traditional contrast all but expunged by the setting was that between trade and usury. Consistent with this, Olivier's costume as Shylock, with morning suit, top hat and cane, enabled him to pass almost as an Antonio.

John Barton's two productions were less explicit in their design than Jonathan Miller's and more eclectic. The Other Place allows little scenery, so the 1978 production did no more than suggest late nineteenth-century Italy and it also set off other resonances. At least two reviewers picked up pre-echoes of fascism, but the main effect was less specific – except that this was a society in which anti-Semitism and female subservience could be taken for granted. The Christians were given to horseplay, pelting each other with bread rolls in the opening scene and shooting off cap pistols and making animal noises in the sequence before Jessica's elopement. According to Benedict Nightingale, 'the shock provoked by their deep, instinctive prejudice is the shock of recognition, because they wear the suits some of our generation's grandfathers wore at public school or Oxbridge' (*New Statesman*, 4 May 1979). Much of the impact of costume and design came, however, from a few small, carefully selected details. Several of the Venetian scenes were played in a seedy café, and Shylock's house had a stand-up counting-house desk. Rarely can large differences of character and position have been suggested so economically as by taste in tobacco. Patrick Stewart, who played Shylock in 1978, recalls that 'Antonio smoked cheroots, Tubal a havana, and Shylock his mean little hand-rolled cigarettes, whose butt-ends were safely stored away for future use' (*Players of Shakespeare*, p. 18).

Barton's 1978 production, like Jonathan Miller's, scarcely differentiated between Venice and Belmont. Both were harsh, even melancholy places, though at the end of Barton's productions the mood changed to hard-won, joyful celebration. Unlike Miller, however, Barton treated the test of the suitors seriously. Neither Morocco nor Arragon was a figure of fun, and Portia had every reason to fear both that they might choose right and that Bassanio might choose wrong. Several critics commented on the intensity of the moments before Bassanio's choice. This was achieved not only by the playing of the scene but by the limited acting area and spare set which focused attention sharply, especially on Portia and her responses. As Roger Warren observed, during Portia's and Bassanio's vows in III ii the ring was 'held up in the hot-spot at the centre; it was similarly held up there when Portia claimed it at the end of the trial scene, the cross-reference helping to begin the transfer back to Belmont' (*Shakespeare Survey 32*, 1979, p. 204).

Some of that intensity had to be sacrificed in 1981 when Barton directed the play on the larger stage of the Royal Shakespeare Theatre. There was partial compensation from the design by Christopher Morley, who had worked on the previous production. This restricted the action to a circular area at the front, spotlit powerfully from overhead, and also enabled visual hints distinguishing Venice from Belmont. Behind the acting area a few props suggested location through a gauzy drape: masts of ships for Venice, with noises off suggesting a harbour, and for Belmont trees – shedding their leaves early on, in rather obvious symbolism, but budding with new life by the end. David Suchet's Shylock in 1981 was a more expansive, less miserly figure than Patrick Stewart's in 1978. He did not roll his own. The behaviour of the Christians was also toned down, and more carefully differentiated. They did not throw bread in the opening scene and played music, rather raucously, instead of cowboy games before Jessica's elopement, though like their predecessors they also made animal noises. Conversely, Barton emphasised Portia's plight even more strongly, to the extent of dressing her in her father's coat to suggest her grief for his loss and having her symbolically roped and covered in a kind of sacrificial cloak for the casket scenes.

Both Jack Gold's television production and John Caird's for the RSC set the play in Renaissance Italy. In keeping with Jonathan Miller's policy as producer of the BBC series, Gold's production does not for the most part attempt a realistic set. Instead Venice is represented by columns, an archway, a bridge, all quite spare and abstract – the columns do not support anything. The most telling visual effect is a dominant tinge of orange, ochre, even red, suitable for Venetian brick but obscurely suggesting oppression and danger. This adds to the contrast between Venice and Belmont which the production stresses. The Belmont scenes take place in a romantic garden complete with gazebo, but again abstract rather than naturalistic. Here the dominant colours are light greens and blues, suggesting cool and leisurely ease – despite Portia's subjection to the caskets. Two exceptions to the abstract design are for indoor scenes: Shylock's house and the Duke's court. The former emphasises Shylock's creed rather than his business, its dark wooden chest bearing a seven-branched candelabrum. The latter is played as a trial in the public court, with at least 30 people present. Again in keeping with Miller's practice for the BBC series, its visual model is in Italian Renaissance painting, the same source as for some of the head-and-shoulders shots of the characters and for their rich, elaborate costumes.

John Caird's production in 1984 was lavish not only in costumes: the set, by Ultz, was sumptuous, suggesting to Paul Allen 'a commercial city which did most of its lucrative business with the East' (*New Statesman*, 20 April 1984). It was a large, tall box occupying the whole stage area, its redbrick walls partly covered by rich red canopies and curtains, its floor carpeted and cushioned. The stage was dominated by two full-size Renaissance pipe-organs whose players remained in place during most of the performance so that they could embellish it with period music. For the quick changes of scene in Act II the organs were moved and rotated, suggesting at one point an oppressive interior for Shylock's house and at another the street in which it stood. Jessica appeared at the top of one of the organs before her escape. Even more surprising was Ultz's contrivance for the caskets. This was a trio of mechanical arms, jointed like monstrous study lamps but supporting large urns on platforms at each one's head. Brought down for the scenes involving Portia, these urns provided almost the only means by which Belmont was distinguished from Venice. When opened up at each suitor's choice they revealed contents of fairground gaudiness and ingenuity: a skeleton with parchment scroll in bony fist, a jack-in-the-box fool's head with an odious wink, and a life-size bust of Portia which for all its qualities failed to justify Bassanio's fulsome praises. When not in use the urns wobbled occasionally in the darkness overhead. They were finally moved back so as to be less conspicuous for the last act, while the curtains above the centre of the stage were withdrawn to suggest a night sky. Costume was no less extravagant than set. The Christians sported many sequins and prominent, bejewelled codpieces. They wore pig masks for the masque scenes. Portia and Nerissa were finely but more tastefully dressed; while Shylock was given something approaching a full stage-Jew treatment. For the final scene the all-white dress of Lorenzo and Jessica promoted a mood of romance.

7 SHYLOCK

Some of the problems facing a modern actor of Shylock have been discussed in Part One. In addition to the tensions and contradictions of the role, and the danger of offering support to anti-Semitism, he somehow needs to cope with the sheer weight of theatrical tradition. The five Shylocks I discuss had to come to terms with all these problems and others too. This they attempted in different ways.

Two of the five used knowledge of Jewish culture and traditions which the play implies – as in Shylock's defence of usury – but does not show directly. Olivier played Shylock as a Jew all but assimilated into a world of merchants and bankers, but in private the symbols of his faith stood out. The doorpost to his house bore the *mezuza*, a small case containing verses to remind Jews of their obligations to God, and Olivier touched a kiss to it when he entered. Similarly, although Olivier's dress was as much the Christian gentleman's as Antonio's, a deeper commitment was brought out when, after vowing revenge to Tubal, he put on the *tallit*, or prayer shawl. This was a gesture to match the line 'Go, Tubal, and meet me at our synagogue' [III i 118–19]. It denied all claim to affinity with the Christians who had betrayed him, reaffirming kinship with his race and faith. When Miller returned to the play as producer of the BBC version, similar use was made of Shylock's home. The interior emphasises Shylock's faith, not his business, with its large wooden chest containing long scrolls and its *menora*, the seven-branched candelabrum of Jewish ritual. While Mitchell plays Shylock with a thickish accent, Olivier's speech suggested an only too consciously naturalised alien. Irving Wardle called it 'a ghastly compound of speech tricks picked up from the Christian rich: posh vowels and the slipshod terminations of the hunting counties' (*Times*, 29 April 1970).

Both Olivier and Mitchell presented Shylock as a man driven much more by emotion than by cash. The 1880s setting helped Olivier in this by virtually removing the distinction between trade and usury. No longer cast as a leech, Olivier could play the offer of the bond as a sardonic, contemptuous joke against a rival's hypocrisy. Miller assisted him further by cutting completely the early aside in which Shylock declares his hatred for Antonio [I iii 38–49]. With the BBC version set in Renaissance Venice and playing the text almost unchanged, Mitchell has to work harder. His main resource is humour and he exploits it brilliantly. This Shylock uses his wry wit both as a shield to prevent hurt and as a means of drawing the Christians into more human contact. He can, just about, shrug off Antonio's insults – he has heard them all before and can reduce them with irony. For him the offer of the bond, accompanied by much laughter, is an attempt to claim kin with those who only half accept him. Taking the words of the text literally, he hopes to gain nothing but Antonio's 'favour' [I iii 165].

Both Olivier's and Mitchell's Shylocks explored the complex relation between kindness and kinship. Jonathan Miller, who was director of the one production and producer of the other, has enlarged on the importance of the theme in interviews with Michael Billington (*Times*, 2 May 1970) and Tim Hallinan (*Shakespeare Quarterly 32*, 1981, p. 142). Both productions suggested that Shylock's offer is part of his effort to belong to a society which excludes him – an effort which goes disastrously wrong when first Jessica leaves and robs him and then Antonio defaults. This is not only an interesting way to explain why Shylock accepts the dinner invitation he had previously refused. It also lends powerful motivation for his rage at Jessica's elopement, since it looks as if Antonio and Bassanio had got him out of the house on purpose. His first words in the aftermath to Salerio and Solanio then carry all the more force: 'You knew, none so well, none so well as you, of my daughter's flight' [III i 22–3]. If this motive is stressed strongly enough, as it was in Miller's productions, it can appear that the shock of grief drives Shylock beside himself into a kind of madness. Such a reading helps explain his terrible alternation of rage and grief in the scene with Tubal and his appalling curses on Jessica. His last lines, asking Tubal to meet him at the synagogue, become an affirmation of the racial and cultural solidarity he had been so foolish as to compromise.

All these effects were powerfully realised by Olivier. They were especially strong in III i, even in the 1973 television version, the highlight of his performance. Because his dress and his manners were so like those of his persecutors the sense of total, unexpected betrayal carried all the more impact. First there was his charge against Salerio and Solanio. They returned a bitter, angry contempt, forcing him to break from them. Then, in an electrifying moment on the words 'Let him look to his bond', repeated with dreadful insistence [III i 43–5], Shylock could be seen seizing the idea of exacting payment in kind. Olivier marked the power of Shylock's passions by pausing before the word in his next speech [54], but he gave the previous word, 'affections', equal weight, emphasising the cause of his fury. The following sequence with Tubal was set inside his house and worked similarly. Shylock caressed a framed photograph of Jessica at the words 'there, there, there, there' [76], only to smash it on the floor; and at the mention of the stolen ring he looked at Leah's portrait, kissed it and collapsed weeping bitterly. All this went to explain the extraordinary frenzy of vengefulness in which he chortled and skipped like a child at the news of Antonio's losses and in which, as malice drew back his lips from his teeth, his face seemed more animal than human. But the final emphasis was again on his suffering. Left alone by Tubal, he stood shrouded in the centre of the room, slowly bowing to his grief.

All Shylocks have to decide when they resolve to exact the forfeit, and it is a tribute to the openness of Shakespeare's play that the range for decision is so wide. No other dramatist – certainly not Marlowe or Jonson – could be imagined allowing such creative discretion. Actors who play Shylock as a villain intend the bond seriously from the first, as did even Henry Irving, renowned for a sympathetic version of the role. But most modern actors place the moment in the same scene as Olivier. For Warren Mitchell it comes even later, at 'Go, Tubal, fee me an officer' [III i 115–16], after a pause following the previous line and its plausible cue, 'But Antonio is certainly undone'. One effect of this is to correct the false, heartless impression given by Salerio and Solanio. The scene in which they mock Shylock's grief contrasts what they see as his inhumanity with Antonio's friendship. Solanio scotches their laughter abruptly with the words: 'Let good Antonio look he keep his day,/Or he shall pay for this' [II viii 25–6]. If Shylock clearly decides to exact payment only later, this emphasises his accusers' prejudice. What tells even more, in the BBC

production, is the disturbing mockery with which the two repay
Shylock's bid for a friendship taken for granted among the
Christians. Trading on that bid, they jostle him with
unpleasant, intimidating familiarity. At his obscene pun,
'Rebels it at these years?' [III i 32–3], Solanio goes so far as to
grasp Shylock by the crotch and heave him up. On his words, 'I
am a Jew' [53], they sardonically fake getting an obvious point
and they supply crude horseplay gestures for most of the
following speech, pointing to eyes, presenting hands, offering
fingers, prodding and tickling him. The scene edges on hysteria
and Shylock is trembling, but with a massive effort he changes
the mood to an appalled silence by shouting the word
'revenge?' [61]. This way of motivating Shylock's fury gains
even more from Tubal. Sometimes played as a closet sadist who
enjoys pitching Shylock from grief at his own losses to delight at
Antonio's, and back again, this Tubal (John Diamond) shows
sympathy and compassion. He tries to calm his friend down,
shushing him and at the terrible curse on Jessica trying to cover
his mouth, murmuring 'no, no'.

The emphasis in these two productions on Shylock's ethnic
identity meant that his response to enforced conversion could
only be one of horror. Olivier collapsed at the sentence and his
stumbling exit was followed by a heart-rending offstage wail.
Mitchell's expression, full face to camera, twists and writhes in
agony, mouth yawning open. The crucifix which Gratiano puts
round his neck and forces him to kiss grips him with revulsion.
Although Shylock never reappears in the play neither
production allowed the audience to forget him in the romance
of Act v. Miller gave the last moment to Jessica, moving off
alone from the others, ill at ease with them and clearly grieving
her father's loss. Over her exit was sung the *Kaddish*, a Jewish
song of mourning. Gold's production is more muted, Jessica
lingering briefly with her deed of gift before leaving the set to
Antonio. What perhaps tells more is the final shot in the trial
scene. This shows Shylock's scales, scabbard and knife on the
table – sad image, in this production, of a vindictiveness which
could be fully understood but which had to be defeated.

It might be argued that Gold's approach, and especially
Miller's, went beyond the words of the play in bringing out
sympathetically Shylock's private life and religion. John

Barton's two productions tried to play down Shylock's Jewishness, in line with his conviction that 'the play is about true and false value and not about race' (letter reproduced in the 1981 programme). Yet in his television series, *Playing Shakespeare*, a difference emerges between the two actors he directed as Shylock. For Patrick Stewart, who played the role in 1978, 'Shylock is an outsider who happens to be a Jew'. But David Suchet, who played Shylock in 1981 and is himself Jewish, rejects this: 'as Shylock I'm not an outsider who *happens* to be a Jew but *because* I'm a Jew' (*Playing Shakespeare*, p. 171). This marks the main difference between his and Stewart's interpretation. While, for instance, Stewart felt no need to play Shylock with a foreign accent, since his language was already so distinctive, Suchet spoke with a slight accent because he felt that Shylock 'was very proud of his Jewishness' (p. 172).

Patrick Stewart has explained that he built his performance of Shylock on a single foundation. His study of the play convinced him that Shylock values money and possessions over people (*Players of Shakespeare*, pp. 15–16). So he played a loner, difficult to reach, using humour and irony 'as a weapon or a smoke-screen or an analgesic' (p. 14). Stewart took pains to convey miserliness. As already noted, he not only rolled but recycled his own straw-thin cigarettes. His dress showed 'an almost studied contempt for neatness or even cleanliness', and inside his house 'the lighting was so dim as to suggest that most of the lightbulbs, or rather candles, had been removed' (pp. 18, 17). It was easy to believe how Lancelot Gobbo could complain of starvation and how his daughter should want to escape. Near the end of ɪɪ v, in which he leaves Jessica in charge of his house, he even slapped her face. Yet for Stewart this was 'consistently the most satisfying scene to play' (p. 22), because in it he could suggest 'a man from whose life love had been removed' (*Playing Shakespeare*, p. 175).

In contrast, David Suchet distinguished between a business and a domestic Shylock. He said in an interview: 'Shylock is a very professional and successful moneylender, but off duty he becomes, in a crazy way, rather childish which can be both endearing and irritating. It is this domestic side that I align with' (*Jewish Chronicle*, Colour Magazine, 19 June 1981). So, although both Shylocks had scales for weighing money in their homes, whereas Stewart struck Jessica Suchet hugged and kissed her. Unlike Stewart, however, Suchet was never satisfied with the scene. Wanting both to express tenderness to his daughter and to show she had reasons for running away, he could not reconcile the contradiction (*Playing Shakespeare*, p. 175). Suchet also distinguished more sharply between his responses to the Christians. He showed 'the minority humour of a man dealing with language and customs not his own', as he described it in the interview, but anger and hatred underneath. Consequently his aside in I iii was direct and shocking. In III i his anger boiled over when, at the climax of his main speech ('Why, revenge!' [64–5]), he grabbed Salerio by the lapel. Better dressed and more confident, Suchet's Shylock could hold his own with the Christians more than Stewart's could. In III iii he did not need to go to Stewart's lengths of sticking up posters and drawing a knife to threaten Antonio. Yet both Shylocks reached at the same time the moment in which they decided to take Antonio's flesh. For both the crucial line was 'I had it of Leah when I was a bachelor' [III i 111–12]. In Stewart's performance the lost ring, embittering happier memories, triggered his vengeful decision. This was a moving glimpse of the vulnerable feelings he had camouflaged and fortified so formidably. In Suchet's it was a reminder of domestic, familial sanctities.

Both Stewart and Suchet played Shylock as a survivor, but in quite different ways. Stewart survived by reducing all emotional commitments to the minimum, expecting nothing and giving nothing. In the trial scene this led to another glimpse of what he had denied in himself. Sure that Portia had been summoned to trick him he was startled off his guard when, at first, she confirmed the bond's legality. His enthusiastic praise gave his feelings away. Yet, the tables turned, he was too hard-bitten to be crushed. Reverting immediately to role, he jumped smartly at the chance offered previously of settling for three times the debt; and, when beaten down much lower, he accepted. His last act, playing the Christians' game, was to laugh louder than anyone at Gratiano's mockery. If he had had to abase himself he had at least saved his life and half his property. In contrast, Suchet survived by passing as a Christian, and in this way his playing of the role recalled

Olivier's. He was never servile but stood on his dignity. The result was to provide a different opportunity in the trial scene. While both actors paused at Portia's word 'charity' [IV i 258], Suchet showed that it not only reached but almost turned him. There was a suggestion that he recognised the evil of what he was doing, and that this enabled him to accept defeat. If so, however, there was a contradiction in the way his awareness was rewarded. At the reminder that he was 'an alien' [346] he shrugged, wryly and wearily. The odds were still stacked against him, nowhere more than in his punishment; but knowing this gave him the dignity not to collapse. He did not need Portia's hand to help him up but left, unbroken, a survivor to the end.

In an interview before the 1984 Stratford production Ian McDiarmid announced his intention of playing Shylock 'as Jewish as I can make him' (*Times*, 9 April 1984). The result raised the question what 'Jewish' might mean. It was an ensemble of ringleted hair, long grey beard, flowing black robes, yellow conical hat and pronounced guttural accent. The performance was equally unrestrained. Vocally, McDiarmid could swoop within a sentence from high-pitched, even falsetto wheedling to sonorous bass, and from whisper to bellow. In gestures too he was abundant, as when he described the 'work of generation' in his 'Laban' speech [I iii 79–85], and when he suited action to words after 'Hath not a Jew eyes?' [III i 53ff.]. Voice and gesture reached a climax when he pitched violently in the sequence with Tubal from joy at Antonio's losses to grief at his own. He rushed to the back of the stage to pull apart the hangings and trumpet out his 'good news', only to be knocked down by the details of Jessica's extravagance. The case for so histrionic a performance is that Shylock puts on an act to ingratiate himself with the Christians and to conceal deep cunning and a rage which breaks out when unguarded. But too often the impression was of a virtuoso stage Jew. Like all the Shylocks discussed, McDiarmid tried to explain his obsession with revenge by his response to what he saw as betrayal. The point was underlined, woodenly, by his giving to Jessica when he said goodbye to her at the end of II v the ring which Tubal later reports her to have squandered. But it might plausibly have been inferred that he intended his malice from the first.

Not only, in I iii, did he march downstage to deliver his hate-filled aside to the audience, but, offering the bond to Antonio, he gave a meaningful pause after 'flesh' and dwelt loweringly on the rest of the sentence [147–8]. It was as if he was throwing down the gauntlet and glad to have it accepted.

McDiarmid's interpretation seems to have been governed by the aim of authenticity, playing what he and the director believed to be the text Shakespeare wrote. This meant setting the play in the Renaissance and doing without what they may have felt to be special pleading for Shylock in previous productions. McDiarmid did not present Shylock as a villain unrelieved. Not only did his behaviour suggest a role Shylock had had to learn, as described above, but he tried to convey suffering and grief as well as malice. This was more convincing when not overdone, as it was in III i. He showed a sting of pain when Antonio responded to his defence of usury with the comment, 'The devil can cite Scripture for his purpose' [I iii 95]. Later, in the trial scene, he stumbled and half fell under the impact of his punishments and yet managed a dignified exit. But the fact that something was awry was shown by laughter in one of the performances I attended: at Shylock's aside in I iii, at his concern over his dream in II v, and most of all at several of Gratiano's tauntings in the trial scene. There is no doubt that neither McDiarmid nor John Caird, the director, intended an anti-Semitic presentation. That such an impression was conveyed – there were protests, such as William Frankel's in *The Times* (17 April 1984) – suggests, at least, miscalculation.

8 PORTIA

With well over 500 lines Portia has the largest part in the play, yet it is named after one of the two characters she defeats and is most famous for the other. Theatre history shows two common fates for the role. One is to be upstaged by Shylock – especially when the final act has been cut, as it often was in the later nineteenth century. The other is to be taken for granted as a paragon of intellect, feeling and eloquence. Both role and play are more complex than either alternative allows. Most recent Portias have tried various ways both of realising the character's complexity and of maintaining a balance of interest with Shylock.

Jonathan Miller's production, however, gave Joan Plowright limited opportunities. Justifying his choice of setting in an interview, he offered nineteenth-century comparisons: to George Eliot's Dorothea and Henry James's Isabel Archer, with their high ideas of themselves, and to the 'emotional frustration of the rich woman living immured like the Lady of Shalott in her tower' (*Times*, 2 May 1970). Yet he did little to bring out these possibilities. Not only did he send up the casket scenes, presenting Morocco and Arragon as comic turns. He also played them down by running Morocco's first scene together with his second. The result was little sense of threat that the wrong husband might claim Portia, especially as Plowright gave her considerable confidence and authority. It was difficult to believe in a mature lady as 'an unlessoned girl' [III ii 159], so she played the line ironically.

Elsewhere also Portia's characterisation was too often subordinated to the demands of the production. In Belmont she was inclined to bossiness, very much the lady of the house. The production rightly emphasised that Jessica is not made very welcome, so Portia could not even remember her name. In Venice, however, though her maturity made her a convincing young lawyer, she behaved more gently. Seated for her speech on mercy, she gave it with quiet straightforwardness, thoughtfully and seriously. When the time came to award judgement she did so reluctantly, as if concerned for Shylock as well as for Antonio. Most of all, the further trap she springs on Shylock came from the Duke: he found another page in the law book she had consulted and passed it on to her for 'The law hath yet another hold on you' [IV i 344]. She dwelt on the word 'alien' [346], glanced disapprovingly several times at the jubilantly vengeful Gratiano, and looked sadly in Shylock's direction as he left. All this reinforced Miller's sympathetic emphasis on Shylock. But it did not wholly square either with Portia's forcefulness in Belmont or with the chances offered by the scene for developing it.

In the BBC production Gemma Jones plays a softer, more
romantic Portia. Older than her companion Nerissa, as was
Plowright's Portia, she shows greater vulnerability – especially
in the casket scenes. This is made easier by the fact that those
scenes are presented more seriously and virtually uncut.
Morocco, no comic butt, is an exotic, heroic figure. He startles
Portia and the others by drawing his scimitar, and later picks
up the golden casket almost as a feat of strength. Arragon has
absurdities of accent and manner, but shows sharp malice in
his discomfiture when he strikes the dwarf in his retinue who
has dropped his gloves. Portia is also helped by the camera,
which, tracking in from each of the choosers, focuses her
anxious responses. What tends to get blurred is the sense that
she is an heiress. A striking example is her transposition of
adjectives in the lines, 'A thousand times more fair, ten
thousand times/More rich' [III ii 154–5]. These lines, here as
they stand in the text, recall Bassanio's emphasis at the end of
the first scene ('In Belmont is a lady richly left,/And she is
fair'). By reversing the adjectives, putting beauty over wealth,
Gemma Jones blunts the play's clear-eyed emphasis on the
material. Similarly this Portia, like Plowright's, simply accepts
Bassanio's easy assumption of the right to welcome new
arrivals to her house.

Because Jones plays Portia less assertively than did
Plowright, there is less difference between her behaviour in
Belmont and in Venice. Again maturity helps her conviction as
a young male lawyer, and again she shows a compassion to
Shylock which is less than explicit in the text. She delivers the
speech on mercy calmly and rationally, not sermonising, she
shows reluctance in confirming judgement, and she looks
painfully after Shylock when he leaves. Elsewhere, however,
she presses the knife back on Antonio's chest when she insists
that Shylock have the justice he demanded ('Therefore prepare
thee to cut off the flesh' [IV i 321]), and she needs no one to tell
her of the Venetian law against aliens – Nerissa passes the
statute book, ammunition prepared in advance. The effect is to
emphasise more sharply than Plowright how Portia hardens her
heart when Shylock refuses all her appeals. But Jones plays the
final scene with a lighter touch. Whereas Plowright made clear
her displeasure with Bassanio by pointedly favouring his friend

('*you* are welcome notwithstanding' [v i 239]), Jones has to conceal some amusement. This finally breaks out on Gratiano's outburst, and she cannot help laughing even when she reproves him for speaking 'grossly' [266]. The reason for the difference in tone is, again, the more romantic approach of Gold's production as compared with Miller's. The latter ended by recalling Shylock through Jessica's sad isolation and, finally, the singing of the Kaddish. In keeping with the policy of the BBC series, which might be described as playing safe with Shakespeare, Gold maintains a comic mood at the end, though giving the final shot to Antonio.

If neither of these productions or performers was quite able to solve the problems of the role, John Barton helped his Portias greatly by making the character central. There were three of them: Marjorie Bland in 1978–9 at The Other Place and the Gulbenkian Studio, Newcastle; then Lisa Harrow in 1979 when the production transferred to the Warehouse; and finally Sinead Cusack in 1981–2. The interpretation behind the role stayed consistent for all three, but by 1981 it had further clarified and developed so it is on Sinead Cusack's performance that I will concentrate.

Barton unified his two productions through the use of specially composed music and his choice of setting and mood – complicating the usual contrast between a romantic Belmont and a worldly, dangerous Venice. Similarly, in her essay on the part Sinead Cusack emphasises how important it was for her to present to the audience the same Portia in the trial scene as at Belmont. The reason she gives is interesting: every time she had seen the play she had 'left the theatre not liking Portia very much' (*Players of Shakespeare*, p. 29). One Portia whom Cusack may not have liked is Judi Dench's in the 1971 Stratford production by Terry Hands. Dubbed 'A Neurotic Portia' in an article by Murray Biggs (*Shakespeare Survey 25*, 1972), she was required by cuts and heavy emphases to overdramatise Portia's concern about the ring her husband gives away.

Cusack's Portia was to be fully sympathetic, and this was achieved in a number of ways. First, Barton's Portias, unlike the previous two discussed, were played very young. Second, and crucially, the casket plot was presented as a nightmare redeemed only by its eventual happy ending. In Portia's first scene Nerissa entered to find her in despair. Still grieving for her father's loss, she could neither face the ordeal of the caskets nor flout his will. Nerissa encouraged her to laugh herself out of her tears by mocking her suitors. Such a way of explaining the mockery is ingenious and in performance it was effective, but Cusack observes: 'this scene caused me more trouble than any other' (*Players of Shakespeare*, p. 33). Neither could it be managed without cuts. The most telling omission was of Portia's rejection of Morocco: 'If he have the condition of a saint and the complexion of a devil, I had rather he should shrive me than wive me' [i ii 123–5]. These lines evidently did not fit the character presented.

Correspondingly both Morocco and Arragon were repellent: the first a fleshy, overbearing voluptuary, the second a heel-clicking Prussian officer. Morocco drew not only his scimitar but his blood, showing how he would make 'incision' for Portia's love [ii i 6], and neither could keep his hands off her. There was little Portia could do about this, because one of the changes introduced in 1981 was to have her roped as well as covered by a kind of penitential cloak. The rope was not tied so its effect was ritual, suggesting a virgin sacrifice just averted. Cusack seems not to have approved, for she records that she got rid of the rope without Barton knowing when the production moved to London (*Players of Shakespeare*, p. 34). Another innovation in both productions was to have Portia sing while Bassanio decides on his choice. This was a dramatic way of bringing out the emotional tension, showing how close Portia is to giving Bassanio the answer while still restrained by obedience to her father's will. When he chose correctly she expressed her relief and liberation by bursting out of her seat and casting all the instruments of her ordeal to the floor. Yet this production, like the others, chose not to emphasise how quickly Bassanio assumes Portia's rights in the house, cutting the part of the speech in which he apologises [iii ii 221–2]. Instead Portia was only too glad to be his prize.

Through her freshness, even naiveté, Barton's Portia was able to keep not only conviction but sympathy in the trial scene. She drew a dry laugh from Shylock almost with her first words ('Which is the merchant here? and which the Jew? [iv i 171]), for Barton made the difference obvious. Equally, she was at first nonplussed by Shylock's refusal of mercy. Patrick Stewart, who played opposite Marjorie Bland and Lisa Harrow, has commented finely on her response, calling it 'pure improvisation':

> She has never imagined that anyone could ask 'why mercy?' or that such a person could exist. She is invited to justify something which is as natural to her as breathing and it is the shock of that which motivates 'The quality of mercy is not strained', and we are moved as we hear her articulate her faith, perhaps for the first time.
>
> (*Players of Shakespeare*, p. 25.)

As Stewart also says, if delivered otherwise the speech becomes a tract – one reason, no doubt, why Cusack was dissatisfied with pre-Barton Portias. Yet the speech is highly formal, even rhetorical, with its balanced clauses and carefully ordered climax; so it is a tribute to the skill of acting and direction that its effect was as Stewart described.

Just as the actor playing Shylock has to decide when he means the bond in earnest, so it was important for Cusack to clarify when Portia can be sure of rendering it null. For her, Portia knows how to defeat Antonio from the start. The reason why she plays the scene out at such length is, she claims,

> to save Shylock, to redeem him – she is passionate to do that. . . . It is only when he shows himself totally ruthless and intractable (refusing even to allow a surgeon to stand by) that she offers him more justice than he desires. (*Players of Shakespeare*, p. 39.)

Again, played like this the scene was dramatically effective. Yet the argument does not wholly satisfy. Cusack distorts the text slightly but revealingly when she says that Shylock will not even allow a surgeon to stand by. What he refuses is to 'Have by some surgeon . . . on your charge' [IV i 254]. As David Nathan remarked, 'One may well ask why the Christians do not provide a surgeon; there's nothing in the bond to prevent them' (*Jewish Chronicle*, 1 May 1981). Second, Portia's words do not in themselves suggest sympathy for Shylock, not least because like the others she most often uses the word 'Jew' both to address and refer to him. Third, even if Shylock rejects every appeal Portia is still inconsistent in denying him the mercy which she has defined as an absolute. For many observers, however, both interpretation and performance were so compelling as to quell any doubts. Portia's behaviour showed compassion, as when, in the 1978 production, she picked up the tobacco tin which Shylock had dropped in his confusion; and when, in 1981, she knelt by him and offered a hand to help him up.

For Cusack the sequence with the rings was 'another painful trial scene' like those with the caskets and with Shylock. In her essay, 'Portia in *The Merchant of Venice*' (pp. 39–40), she says she played it too seriously, but her emphasis contributed to the production's unity, further confirmed the centrality of Portia and enabled a strong sense of difficulties overcome. There was no reminder of Shylock, so firmly had it been stressed that he was defeated on his own terms and that Portia deserved her victories. The production ended joyfully, almost festally, with cheering, embracing and finally all the characters joining to sing in unison.

The tone of John Caird's production at Stratford in 1984 was quite different, and Frances Tomelty took the risk of playing Portia less sympathetically. Some phrases from three of the reviews on 12 April after the press night give the flavour of the responses she evoked: 'a confident, insensitive bachelor girl' (Irving Wardle, *Times*), 'an intense, hard-driven quality' (Martin Hoyle, *Financial Times*), 'unusually vehement and strong willed' (Michael Billington, *Guardian*). This was not a youthful Portia but one who had reached years of discretion without full power to exercise it. Despite her self-possession she bridled at the constraints of her father's will, and she showed both superiority and contempt when mocking her suitors to Nerissa. Like Gold's BBC production, Caird's made a comic figure of Arragon but not of Morocco. Arragon was a fop, costumed with absurd extravagance, but Morocco was tall, slim and dignified – except when his deadpan 'O hell! What have we here?' on opening the golden casket brought an unavoidable laugh from the audience [II vii 62]. Nevertheless, in keeping with the distaste Portia shows in the text for a black suitor, she winced when he kissed her hand at the words 'my gentle queen' [II i 12]. For the casket scenes she knelt at the front facing the audience, suggesting not so much a victim's passivity as the detachment of one who could not bear to watch what she could do nothing to influence. After Antonio's letter had been read out she played the words 'O love' [III ii 322] not as addressing Bassanio but as a comment, suggesting painful knowledge bought by experience.

Portia's betrothal to Bassanio was a solemn love ceremony, almost static until broken into by the trouble over the bond. In contrast, her next scene was much livelier. She showed enjoyment not only at her liberation but especially at the prospect of taking on a male role to go to Venice. Her behaviour in the trial scene was also unconventional. She gave the famous speech on mercy gently, sententiously, but with some condescension, yet showed little sympathy for Shylock. John Peter exaggerated in speaking of her 'cold, fearsome efficiency' (*Sunday Times*, 15 April 1984), but it was certainly a deliberate, concentrated performance. She read from a large volume the clauses which foil Shylock. In the final scene she showed some of the same qualities, enjoying Bassanio's discomfiture. This was a lady who knew her rights as well as what was right, and was determined to have them. Her point carried, she could show magnanimity and she extended a hand to Antonio as the scene closed. But it was clear that none of the men in the play was her match.

9 INTERPRETATION AND UNITY

Special problems face all modern productions of Shakespeare. One, as with any play from a different period or culture, is the gap in knowledge and experience between the audiences for whom the plays were written and those today. A second is the weight of tradition – so many of the plays boast famous productions, or performances, in the past. Then there is competition in the present to produce new and arresting performances which will fill seats. Companies which hope to attract tourists and school parties have the further need to stage productions which will be clear as well as entertaining. The BBC Shakespeare series, designed to carry broad, lasting appeal for worldwide marketing, has set itself much the same aims.

These pressures, and others, encourage productions unified by single interpretations. The same tendency is strongly reinforced both by the power of the director, usually extensive, and by received academic and theatrical wisdom. In turn, to unify a production, and convey an interpretation effectively, it usually helps to alter the text. Very few productions present unchanged the texts we know as Shakespeare's, and some go well beyond occasional cuts to omit, reposition or even write in whole sequences. Other ways of shaping productions include setting, design and costume, pacing, casting and characterisation – both of individual roles and of their parts in the whole. Some of these are the stuff of theatre, others have long been accepted. With the exception of writing in new sequences, all were exploited in the productions discussed.

Two of the productions unified the play thematically. In 1978 and 1981 the theme John Barton made central was 'true and false value' – representing the modern academic consensus about the play, so far as there is one. The alternative view, now held by a minority, is that the play is about race. This, with considerable subtlety, was Jonathan Miller's emphasis in 1970. His own phrase 'kith and kin' best defines it (*Times*, 2 May 1970). The other two productions were unified more by approach. Although Jack Gold's BBC version, with Miller as producer, develops in its own way the theme of 'kith and kin', its main approach is that of romantic comedy. Finally, the basis of John Caird's production at Stratford in 1984 was historical. It used a Renaissance setting but did not limit itself to what it took as Renaissance attitudes. The contrast in these productions between unity by theme and unity by approach parallels the contrast between updated and Renaissance settings. This suggests that it is easier to unify a play thematically if it is taken out of its historical context.

No production has unified *The Merchant of Venice* more successfully than John Barton's. The confined area of The Other Place, where the production began in 1978, gave it discipline and concentration. Then, as I have shown, Barton took pains to ensure that Shylock did not dominate the play and that Portia's role was not only central but consistent and

1. 'A man from whose life love had been removed' with Shylock (Patrick Stewart) and Jessica (Avril Carson) in John Barton's 1978 RSC production.
Photograph © Joe Cocks Studio

2. 'The Jew shall have all justice' with Shylock (David Suchet), Bassanio (Jonathan Hyde) and Portia (Sinead Cusack) in John Barton's 1981 RSC production.
Photograph © Donald Cooper

3. 'And here choose I' with Bassanio (Jonathan Hyde) and Portia (Sinead Cusack) in John Barton's 1981 RSC production.
Photograph © Donald Cooper

4. 'The curse never fell upon our nation till now' with Shylock (Ian McDiarmid) in John Caird's 1984 RSC production.
Photograph © Donald Cooper

5. 'Kith and Kin' with Shylock (Warren Mitchell) in the 1980 BBC-TV production. Photograph © BBC Copyright Photograph

sympathetic. He also drew together the different parts of the play by suggesting that Venice and Belmont were parallels, not opposites. Accordingly there was not one trial scene but three: Bassanio's test complementing Shylock's and, finally, Antonio's when he has to acknowledge Portia's rightful victory ('My soul upon the forfeit' [v i 252]) in pledging his friend's faith. One result, clearly intended though puzzling to some reviewers, was that Shylock's trial was played down. In keeping with the view that this scene represents not a trial as such but 'a hearing in chambers or a final, private appeal' (*Players of Shakespeare*, p. 24), informality was the keynote. During it coffee was served in the 1978 production – the Duke even pouring for Shylock – and sherry in 1981.

Altogether the effect of these emphases was to alter decisively the balance of the play as many have understood it. As Michael Billington said, 'Instead of seeming, as so often, a failed tragedy the play becomes a genuine comedy in which the characters progress to some kind of spiritual understanding' (*Guardian*, 23 April 1981). Remarkably, the 1981 production suggested that neither Shylock nor Antonio was wholly excluded from this, Shylock half-admitting the appeal to 'charity' and Antonio giving up to Portia his claim on his friend. Gareth Lloyd-Evans put it rather strongly when he said that through Portia the characters had 'realised themselves' (*Stratford-upon-Avon Herald*, 1 May 1981). Shylock did not retract his intentions and paid the penalty, Gratiano stayed boorish and bigoted to the end, and Antonio's final gesture was to remove the garland which Portia had placed round his neck. Yet, thanks to Portia, both Bassanio and Lorenzo had clearly matured beyond their earlier easy materialism. The point was underlined at the end when the whole company chorused the song which Portia had sung before Bassanio's choice, 'Tell me where is fancy bred'. This was a simple and effective way to underline the production's theme.

In his 1970 production Jonathan Miller relied much more than Barton on design and setting to reinforce his theme. By narrowing the differences between Shylock and the Christians he threw into relief the importance of Shylock's race. Shylock and Antonio were similarly dressed – so that Portia's question, 'Which is the merchant here? and which the Jew?' [iv i 171], was quite natural. But the production also virtually eliminated the distinction between trade and usury implicit in Portia's question and explicit elsewhere in the play. Not that this was only a matter of setting. Barton, too, set his production in the late nineteenth century but he did not minimise such differences, especially with Patrick Stewart's Shylock. Because he emphasised the setting much less he was able to get away with the historical contradiction that usury had long become accepted. Shylock was presented with the symbols of his business and the miser's – usurer's – instinct was attributed to his character. Miller developed an opposite view with his theme of 'kith and kin'. Not only was Shylock excluded, despite an assimilation apparently all but complete. The production showed him as warped and finally destroyed by the society in whose mirror he had dressed.

In some ways Miller's detailed setting created problems. It was impossible to imagine so gentlemanly a Shylock carving flesh from Antonio so he had two followers in the trial scene ready to do it for him. In the ATV version directed by John Sichel his knife-whetting is minimised; in the theatre the task was given to one of his assistants. Similarly, Shakespeare's bawdry did not come easily from a Victorian lady. Portia's role was also influenced by the emphasis given to Shylock. She handled him with a gentleness and compassion less evident in her behaviour elsewhere in the play, for instance to her unwelcome suitors and to Jessica. Though it might better have suited the production's theme if she had joined in the baiting, the idea of a romantic heroine was upheld – at some strain.

Jack Gold's production, with its Renaissance setting, avoids contradiction between speech and speaker but the unity it achieves is questionable. On the one hand it develops the 'kith and kin' theme of Miller's 1970 production. There is much physical contact and much humour, but where Shylock is concerned this good fellowship is a sham. He is admitted to it when he is needed, only to be shown his error when things go wrong. The point is sharpened by the intimate focus of television. In conflict with this, however, is the production's romantic approach elsewhere. Though it shows up the nauseous attitudes and behaviour of Gratiano, Salerio and Solanio it takes Bassanio at his own word ('innocence' [I i 145]) and sentimentalises Antonio. Most of all, it takes money for granted – much as Portia does, unavailingly, in offering any amount for the bond. I have mentioned how Gemma Jones switches the words 'fair' and 'rich' when she dedicates herself to Bassanio. Similarly, Bassanio shows no sign of needing Antonio's loan. His costume is resplendent from the start and he does not change it for Belmont.

Jessica and Lorenzo are also treated romantically. In an interview about the BBC series Jonathan Miller suggested a parallel between Jessica and Portia, each escaping a father's will (*Shakespeare Quarterly 32*, 1981, p. 142). This helps motivate Jessica's desertion – always a problem when Shylock is played sympathetically. Shylock's home is dark and gloomy, in keeping with his puritanical attitudes, and Jessica longs to escape it. She and Lorenzo are presented as counterparts on a lower, fleshlier level to Portia and Bassanio. The innuendoes traded by the two leave no doubt about what has brought them together, as when Jessica looks downward at the word 'renew' and says she would 'out-night' Lorenzo [v i 14, 23]. The trouble with this is that it conflicts with the play's suggestion that Jessica may not join Christian society so easily. Miller conveyed that suggestion in 1970, as I have said, but by 1980 his view seems to have shifted. The later emphasis fits the production's romantic approach. But it sits uneasily with the sympathetic treatment of Shylock.

Underlying John Caird's production was an idea of *The Merchant of Venice* in its historical setting. I have described the rich set with its Renaissance pipe-organs and its luxury suggesting Eastern trade. Further details included authentic Renaissance music, hunchbacks for Lancelot and his father in keeping with scholarly suggestion (e.g. Penguin edition, p. 179), and six pages of quotations in the original programme demonstrating historical attitudes to Jews and to usury. Similarly, in presenting Shylock director and actor seem to have aimed at the kind of figure which some scholars of the period have conjectured, with most though not all of the attributes of a conventional stage Jew.

As Shylock Ian McDiarmid tried to convey the human being beneath the stereotype, pulling out all the emotional stops in his anger and grief. Correspondingly Bassanio's friends were

flashy, insensitive young bloods with a need for money and a
taste for racial abuse. For the scene of Jessica's escape they
wore pig masks and later, in II viii, Solanio wore a caricature
mask of a Jew. But the nastiness of the anti-Semitism did not
come through in the way apparently intended. The audience
found Gratiano, played by the personable James Simmons,
rather attractive. Amanda Root's lively Jessica encouraged
support for her rebellion, countenanced in turn by the romantic
mood given to her midnight idyll in Belmont with Lorenzo.
Most of all, the production had too few resources to call in
question the Jewish stereotypes it presented. This might have
been corrected in part by stressing Antonio's malice. But
Christopher Ravenscroft played the role limply, even half-
fainting when in the trial scene all appeared lost.

The production may have owed something to modern
feminism as well as to assumptions about Renaissance
attitudes. Portia was very obviously at the mercy of male
contrivance as the urns homed in from above, and as a ghostly
offstage voice intoned the inscriptions and the song before
Bassanio chose. Like the other Christians Bassanio seemed
thoughtless rather than heartless, and despite his solemn face
in the casket scene it was a mystery how he chose correctly.
Nevertheless Portia got the man she wanted, put down her
other suitors adeptly and taught both Shylock and Antonio
firm lessons. Yet, just as robot-controlled urns clashed with the
Renaissance set, so the conceptions of Portia and Shylock never
meshed. The production had the worst of both worlds in the
trial scene, for neither her triumph nor his defeat demanded
sympathy. There was a smaller-scale example of the same
self-cancelling tendency with Nerissa. Caird took literally a
name usually accepted as meaning 'dark-haired' by casting in
the role Josette Simon who is handsomely dark-skinned.
Perhaps the intention was to draw a racist sting. If so, the
production failed to follow through. Portia's warmth towards
her companion and her sneer at Morocco's colour ('Let all of
his complexion choose me so' [II vii 79]) presented a
meaningless contradiction. In his collage of the play Charles
Marowitz also casts Nerissa as black, but his stage direction
after Portia's gibe calls for an exchange of looks, 'registering the

fact that Portia has committed a faux pas in relation to her black companion' (*The Marowitz Shakespeare*, 1978, p. 252).

The problems of Caird's production were partly of its own making, such as the empty, mechanical luxury of the set. Similarly, by playing up the issue of race, both in Shylock's presentation and at length in the programme, the production raised more questions than can have been intended. The original programme had to be revised, presumably at considerable expense, so that its lavish illustration of anti-Semitic attitudes did not offend. Fundamentally, however, the production found no convincing path through the play's difficulties. It brought out, for instance, the harsh side there is to Portia – exactly what John Barton and Sinead Cusack had to work so hard to suppress. But it failed to integrate this.

The problem is how to present the play's tensions and contradictions without either perplexing them further, as Caird did, or dissolving them away. None of the other productions struck the balance quite successfully. The two that came nearest were Jonathan Miller's and John Barton's. Miller added some irreconcilables while removing others, but the result was consistently stimulating. Barton resolved the play's complexities within a single interpretation, aided by his rehearsal process which develops individual characters in isolation (*Players of Shakespeare*, p. 32). The BBC version, with its rich portraits and romantic comedy, is too often bland when Shylock is off screen.

The Merchant of Venice used to be known as a play that cannot fail in the theatre. The reason is that it was once possible to take its contradictions for granted. Belmont could be milked for romance and mystery, both Belmont and Venice for impressive settings. If played as the villain of a sophisticated melodrama, Shylock could reassure conventional certainties and prejudices. If played for sentiment, reassurance could be even more comforting, for the audience was also offered an image of its own supposed tolerance. Caird's production illustrates how difficult it is now to stage the play responsibly. But a unified approach is not necessarily a better solution. If the nature of the play is to ask questions, those questions need to carry their full weight.

10   ALTERNATIVES

In Chapter 5 I suggested that *The Merchant of Venice* is one of
Shakespeare's 'Plays Unpleasant'. This is borne out by several
of the productions discussed, especially Jonathan Miller's and
for very different reasons John Caird's. In conclusion I will
consider some more radical responses to the problems the play
presents.

Charles Marowitz's version, *Variations on the Merchant of
Venice*, was first staged in 1977. In his work with the Open Space
Theatre Marowitz had produced dramatic collages of several
Shakespeare plays, including *Hamlet, Macbeth* and *Measure for
Measure*. He has collected these in *The Marowitz Shakespeare*, and
in the introduction he explains his motives for adapting *The
Merchant of Venice*:

> What had always angered me about *Merchant* was that
> contemptible trial scene in which Shylock is progressively
> humiliated, stripped of all property and dignity and sent packing
> from the courtroom a forced convert, a disreputable father, an
> unmasked villain. It was to try to redress this balance that I decided
> to reorder *Merchant* and 'vary' its moral implications.   (p. 22.)

Marowitz set about this by locating the play in Palestine during
British occupation in 1948. Antonio becomes a diplomat
responsible for restricting Jewish immigration and so forcing
many Jews trying to escape from Europe into concentration
camps. Bassanio and the other Venetians become British
officers and Portia a fat-cat heiress; while the Jews (Marowitz
gave a small part to Chus, only mentioned in Shakespeare's
play) are all committed nationalists, Shylock holding a
respectable place in the community. The casket scenes are sent
up by an hilarious process of elimination in which Bassanio
disguises himself first as Morocco then as Arragon to arrive
finally at the right answer. Marowitz also not only cut and re-
positioned speeches and whole sequences but included extracts
from Marlowe's *The Jew of Malta*. Jessica, combined with
Marlowe's Abigail, becomes a faithful Zionist who marries
Lorenzo at her father's instruction. Deceiving the British, this

provides a false but plausible motive for Shylock's determination to exact the bond. Marowitz's play culminates, and ends, with the trial scene. The Marlowe extracts not only enable Shylock to defy his persecutors more directly – especially when Arragon's speech about unrewarded merit is also transferred to him [II ix 39–49]. Chus, cast as a terrorist, has the words of Marlowe's Barabas telling the Governor that the garrison has been mined (*The Jew of Malta*, v v 26–33, in *Christopher Marlowe: The Complete Plays*, ed. J. B. Steane, [Harmondsworth, 1969]). The scene ends with Shylock's famous speech, 'Hath not a Jew eyes?' [III i 49–66]. Then Shylock leaves for the guerrillas to gun down their oppressors and dynamite the building.

Even this brief account of Marowitz's adaptation suggests that it creates as many problems as it solves. Although, for instance, it succeeds in casting Shylock's enemies unambiguously as oppressors, in doing so it might be seen as justifying terrorism. Such a charge does not have to be conceded if the aim is to raise questions about the original play and its relation to history, recent as well as distant. But the central issue is whether the play itself might not be performed so as to raise such questions more effectively.

Arnold Wesker is one of those who would deny both this possibility and the usefulness of adapting Shakespeare's text. He found Jonathan Miller's National Theatre production as unpleasant as any other and he has described how, watching it, he was struck by what he saw as the play's 'irredeemable anti-semitism' (*Guardian*, 29 August 1981). His comment was occasioned by John Barton's production to which he also objected strongly. Believing the play to be anti-Semitic, Wesker maintains that no production can be justified whatever the good intentions of director, cast or critics. His own response had been to write a completely different play, *The Merchant* (*Plays Volume 4*, 1980), using the same basic materials. Jewish himself, he wanted to show the Venetian ghetto with more historical accuracy than Shakespeare as a place of culture and humanity; and to present the flesh-bond as a pledge of humorous friendship which went disastrously wrong. In it Shylock is a bibliophile, not a leech. His exaction of the bond is determined by the stark obligation to uphold the laws of

Venice, which alone guarantee the safety of his community. Wesker's play was first performed in Stockholm (1976), later in New York (1977) and Birmingham (1978); it has yet to be staged in London.

Wesker argues that there is no point in presenting Shakespeare's play as a product of its time, for that is not the time we live in. But there is another reason against this. It has proved too easy to take the play for granted – to fall short of recognising the questions it sets. Ridiculously, *The Merchant of Venice* has long been considered a safe introduction to Shakespeare and it has been a staple of British school and examination syllabi. Its popularity in the theatre has also owed much to productions that have reinforced prejudices. But it is wrong, and dangerously condescending, to beg questions about the nature of the play and its first audiences. What it offers is not the spectacle of a dangerous prejudice from which we are now emancipated. Racism is far from dead and Shylock is not the whole play. Instead the potential reward is the play's tense, contradictory grappling with problems of values, gender and race. Springing as it does from anti-Semitic attitudes, Shakespeare's *Merchant* keeps more than an historical interest because of its ability to put those attitudes and others in question.

Productions which realise this quality of the play most successfully have to be prepared to take risks. Jonathan Miller's for the National Theatre is the best example among those discussed. Another example I have seen was a brilliantly inventive production by Simon Shepherd at Nottingham University in 1980. As on the Elizabethan stage this was performed with little scenery and mainly in modern costume. Properties and a few distinctive items of dress counted all the more by their power of suggestion. Bassanio was a youthful Pierrot figure, suggesting a Nijinsky to Antonio's sombre, dinner-suited Diaghilev. Portia was a mature lady made languid by wealth and subjection who asserted herself vehemently when freed. She thumped the table when she hectored out her famous speech on mercy, and imperiously called all the shots in the closing scene. The casket scenes were frivolously treated but very funny. Two retainers, increasingly knackered, performed physical jerks as each suitor gave his

speech, conveying the element of absurd ordeal in the ritual.
While Bassanio chose, Gratiano and Nerissa made up to each
other in the background and added to the ludicrous comedy –
though also preparing for Gratiano's marriage request.

In contrast to all this hilarity Shylock was played wholly
straight. He was a man of stern rectitude, with no accent, no
mannerisms and, except for an ordinary leather coat, no
distinctive dress. Left behind after the trial scene, the coat was a
spare reminder of his absence as the Christians blandly
celebrated. The production showed with powerful conviction
the force of institutionalised prejudice – also brought out in
Jessica's discomfort, ribaldly welcomed for her looks and her
money but later left to linger on the sidelines in embarrassment.
But the playing of Shylock was so strong that his capitulation to
Portia came as a surprise. It seemed more likely that he would
exact his penalty from Antonio in a kind of judicial suicide
mission. This shows how far the production had reworked the
play and perhaps suggests what sort of limits apply to such
reworking.

But there is another possible approach, which the
production tried more tentatively. The five main productions I
have discussed all assumed that the play creates 'realistic'
characters. Those taking part in and discussing the
productions often talked as if the characters were actual,
individual people. This way of thinking is so familiar that it is
difficult to recognise its artificiality. Yet, although
Shakespeare's plays present deeply convincing impressions of
human behaviour, it is unlikely that he aimed at realistic
illusions of character in the modern sense. Such an assumption
stems from stage conventions which developed after the
introduction of the proscenium stage in the Restoration and the
rise of naturalistic theatre two centuries later. It is supported by
the acting method that encourages performers to get into the
skins of the characters. So, for example, when John Barton's
two Shylocks talk about playing the inconsistencies of the role
to the full, there is an inbuilt limit to these. They will eventually
come together in a rich, complex portrait of the human being
illuminated (*Playing Shakespeare*, p. 174). Such an emphasis
makes for highly effective drama. It is also in keeping with
Barton's view that *The Merchant of Venice* is not an anti-Semitic

play and that Shylock is not representative of his race. But the notion of individuality linked to that of 'realistic' characters, and usually taken for granted today, is also anachronistic as applied to Shakespeare. It is rooted in liberal, bourgeois thinking which emphasises what it sees as each person's freedom to take his or her own economic and moral decisions.

Against this there is an alternative tradition represented in the twentieth century by Brecht's alienation technique and, despite the apparent paradox, more consistent with Elizabethan practice. In this kind of theatre, as on the Elizabethan stage, there is no artificial barrier between audience and performers. Consequently the stage illusion can be broken with ironic or critical effect – especially when a speaker moves downstage to engage the audience directly. Such an approach might be of special value to *The Merchant of Venice*. It would bring out Shakespeare's double-edged treatment of the stage Jew stereotype as described in the article by Alan C. Dessen which I discussed in Chapter 4. Even more important, it would focus sharply the contradictions shown up by the play in matters of gender as well as race. For example, two of the play's most famous speeches, Shylock's 'Hath a Jew eyes?' and Portia's 'The quality of mercy', might both be played to the audience, forcing home the moral and political questions they raise. The result would not be Shakespeare as understood traditionally. But, as traditional Shakespeare is largely a nineteenth-century creation, that should not worry us. Its reward might be a renewed understanding of a play rarely out of the repertory or the syllabus, but too often thanks to complacency.

READING LIST

Critical editions available in paperback include: New Penguin, ed. W. Moelwyn Merchant (Penguin Books, Harmondsworth, 1967); Signet, ed. Kenneth Myrick (New American Library, New York and London, 1965); and New Arden, ed. John Russell Brown (Methuen, London and New York, repr. 1961). The New Variorum edition by H. H. Furness (1888, Dover paperback, New York, 1964) indicates textual variants and is a mine of pretwentieth-century criticism. Charles Marowitz's *Variations on the Merchant of Venice* is included in *The Marowitz Shakespeare* (Marion Boyars, London; Drama Book Specialists, New York, 1978). Arnold Wesker's *The Merchant* is included in *Plays Volume 4* (Penguin Books, Harmondsworth, 1980) and has been edited with commentary and notes by Glenda Leeming (Methuen, London, 1983).

SOURCES AND BACKGROUND

The New Variorum and Arden editions provide extracts from the probable main sources, but the fullest account is in Geoffrey Bullough, *Narrative and Dramatic Sources of Shakespeare*, Vol. 1 (Routledge, London; Columbia UP, New York, 1964). Edgar Rosenberg, *From Shylock to Svengali* (Stanford UP, Stanford, 1960; Peter Owen, London, 1961) is a stimulating account of Jewish stereotypes in post-medieval English literature.

SURVEYS AND COLLECTIONS OF CRITICISM

The best survey is Gāmini Salgādo's, 'The Middle Comedies', in Stanley Wells (ed.), *Shakespeare: Select Bibliographical Guides* (Oxford UP, London and New York, 1973). Norman Rabkin discusses much of the criticism on the play in 'Meaning and *The Merchant of Venice*', *Shakespeare and the Problem of Meaning* (Chicago UP, Chicago and London, 1981).

The best collection of essays is by John Wilders (ed.), *Shakespeare: The Merchant of Venice* (Macmillan Casebook Series, London and Basingstoke; Aurora Publications, Nashville, Tenn., 1969). This is partly complemented by Sylvan Barnet (ed.), *Twentieth-Century Interpretations of The Merchant of Venice* (Prentice-Hall, Englewood Cliffs, N.J., 1970).

CRITICISM

Note: asterisks (*) indicate material represented in the *Casebook* edited by John Wilders.

*W. H. Auden, 'Brothers and Others', *The Dyer's Hand* (Random House, New York, 1962; Faber, London, 1963). Brilliant and provocative.
*C. L. Barber, 'The Merchants and the Jew of Venice', *Shakespeare's Festive Comedies* (Princeton UP, Princeton, 1959). Thematic reading about use of riches, touching on play's ambivalence.
Ralph Berry, 'Discomfort in *The Merchant of Venice*', *Shakespeare and the Awareness of the Audience* (Macmillan, London and Basingstoke; St Martin's Press, New York, 1985). On presentation of social tensions, and their communication to the audience.
*John Russell Brown, 'Love's Wealth and the Judgement of *The Merchant of Venice*', *Shakespeare and his Comedies*, 2nd edition (Methuen, London, 1962; Barnes and Noble, New York, 1968). Mainstream thematic reading.
*Sigurd Burckhardt, '*The Merchant of Venice*: The Gentle Bond', *ELH 29* (1962), pp. 239–62. Bond as controlling metaphor, linking Venice and Belmont.
Nevill Coghill, 'The Basis of Shakespearian Comedy' (1950), Anne Ridler (ed.), *Shakespeare Criticism 1935—1960* (Oxford UP, London and Toronto, 1963). Influential exposition of Mercy/Justice reading.
Lawrence Danson, *The Harmonies of The Merchant of Venice* (Yale UP, New Haven and London, 1978). Academic interpretation on Christian lines.
Alan C. Dessen, 'The Elizabethan Stage Jew and Christian Example', *Modern Language Quarterly 35*, 1974, pp. 231–45. Shakespeare's plays in context of other Elizabethan dramas dealing with Jew as moral type.
René Girard, ' "To Entrap the Wisest": A Reading of *The Merchant of Venice*', *Literature and Society*, ed. Edward W. Said (Johns Hopkins UP, Baltimore and London, 1980). Shylock as scapegoat, thematically or structurally according to nature of audience.
*Harold C. Goddard, '*The Merchant of Venice*', *The Meaning of Shakespeare* (Chicago UP, Chicago, 1951). Resourceful, at times over-ingenious, ironic reading.
*Harley Granville-Barker, *Prefaces to Shakespeare*, 2nd series (Sidgwick and Jackson, London, 1930). Still useful though now rather dated.
Frank Kermode, 'The Mature Comedies', John Russell Brown and Bernard Harris (eds), *Early Shakespeare* (Arnold, London, 1961; Capricorn Books, New York, 1966). Unabashed thematic reduction.
Alexander Leggatt, '*The Merchant of Venice*', *Shakespeare's Comedy of Love* (Methuen, London; Barnes and Noble, New York, 1973). Interesting on relation between conventional pattern and 'detailed humanity'.
Barbara K. Lewalski, 'Biblical Allusion and Allegory in *The Merchant of Venice*', *Shakespeare Quarterly 13*, 1962, pp. 327–43. Relentless allegorical interpretation.
*Graham Midgley, '*The Merchant of Venice*: A Reconsideration', *Essays in*

Criticism 10, 1960, pp. 119–33. Play as 'a twin study in loneliness', with Antonio as 'unconscious homosexual' balancing Shylock.

A. D. Moody, *Shakespeare: The Merchant of Venice* (Arnold, London, 1964). The best short study, though inclined to over-emphasise irony.

D. J. Palmer, '"The Merchant of Venice", or the Importance of Being Earnest', M. Bradbury and D. J. Palmer (eds), *Shakespearian Comedy* (Arnold, London, 1972; Holmes and Meier, New York, 1979). Subtle essay on how dramatic action appeals to primary affections over moral arguments.

*E. C. Pettet, '*The Merchant of Venice* and the Problem of Usury', *Essays and Studies 31*, 1945, pp. 19–33. Romantic reading based on discussion of Elizabethan attitudes to usury.

James Smith, 'The Merchant of Venice', *Shakespearian and other essays* (Cambridge UP, Cambridge and New York, 1974). Ironic reading, finding luck rather than logic in casket scenes.

STAGE HISTORY

John Barton, 'Exploring a Character: Playing Shylock', *Playing Shakespeare* (Methuen, London and New York, 1984). Account originally presented on TV of creating Shylock's role with Patrick Stewart and David Suchet.

Murray Biggs, 'A Neurotic Portia', *Shakespeare Survey 25*, 1972, pp. 153–59. Critical attack on Terry Hands' 1971 RSC production.

Philip Brockbank (ed.), *Players of Shakespeare* (Cambridge UP, Cambridge and New York, 1985). Essays by two performers in John Barton's RSC productions: Sinead Cusack, 'Portia in *The Merchant of Venice*', and Patrick Stewart, 'Shylock in *The Merchant of Venice*'.

John Russell Brown, 'Creating a Role: Shylock', *Shakespeare's Plays in Performance* (Arnold, London, 1966; St Martin's Press, New York, 1969). Survey of the history of the role.

Hugh Hunt, *Old Vic Prefaces* (Routledge, London, 1954; Greenwood Press, Westport, Conn., 1973). Records a conventional but skilful romantic production.

Toby Lelyveld, *Shylock on the Stage* (Western Reserve UP, Cleveland, 1960; Routledge, London 1961). Thorough, detailed history of the role.

Arthur C. Sprague, *Shakespeare and the Actors* (Harvard UP, Cambridge, 1944; Russell and Russell, New York, 1963). Summarises various performances of Shylock.

J. C. Trewin, *Going to Shakespeare* (Allen and Unwin, London, 1978). Reminiscences of various post-war productions.

Arnold Wesker, 'Why I Fleshed out Shylock', *Distinctions* (Cape, London, 1985). Reprint of *Guardian* article putting case against play and outlining own alternative.

INDEX OF NAMES